# Succeed in IELTS Life Skills

**CEFR**

## Speaking & Listening

**Download for FREE** the Audio files and the Audioscript.
Use this link:
http://www.globalelt.co.uk/Succeed-IELTS-LIFE-SKILLS-A1.html

**STUDENT'S BOOK**

Andrew Betsis
Lawrence Mamas

GlobalELT

# IELTS Life Skills – Level A1

## What's in the IELTS Life Skills test?
Face-to-face Speaking and Listening test
You will take the test with *an examiner*, and with *one other candidate*.
The tasks in IELTS Life Skills are designed to reflect the *everyday experience of communicating* in an English-speaking country.

### Phase 1a
Answer personal questions on different subject areas such as work, study etc. **4-5 min**

### Phase 1b
Ask your partner some questions on a topic given by the examiner. When you are finished, your partner will ask you questions on a different topic. You have 1 and a half minute to prepare for this phase. **5 min**

### Phase 2a
Listen to 2 short recordings. First, listen for the general topic and choose an answer from 3 options. Then, listen again for 2 pieces of specific information in order to answer the examiner's questions. **4 min**

### Phase 2b
You are given a topic to talk about with your partner. This is a general discussion where you share ideas and opinions. **3-4 min**

**Total Time 16-18 min**

*Short discussions* on *everyday subjects* including:

- Personal details / Experiences
- Family and friends
- Buying goods
- Work
- Health
- Leisure
- Education / Training
- Transport
- Housing
- Weather.

You will be expected to:
- *listen and respond* to spoken language, including simple narratives, statements, questions and single-step instructions
- *communicate* basic information, feelings and opinions on familiar topics
- *talk with another person* in a familiar situation about familiar topics.

Tasks may include:
- describing
- giving opinions
- giving personal information
- stating preferences
- commenting
- asking for information or descriptions
- agreeing and disagreeing
- explaining, giving reasons or justifying
- deciding
- suggesting
- selecting

Published by GLOBAL ELT LTD
www.globalelt.co.uk
Copyright © **GLOBAL ELT LTD, 2015**

Andrew Betsis and Lawrence Mamas
Contributors: Marianna Georgopoulou, Sean Haughton, Panou Despoina and Varvara Vallianatou

Every effort has been made to trace the copyright holders and we apologize in advance for any unintentional omission.
We will be happy to insert the appropriate acknowledgements in any subsequent editions.

All rights reserved. No part of this publication may be reproduced, stored in a retrieval system, or transmitted in any form or by any means, electronic, mechanical, photocopying, recording or otherwise, without the prior permission in writing of the Publisher. Any person who does any unauthorised act in relation to this publication may be liable to criminal prosecution and civil claims for damages.

- Succeed in IELTS Life Skills - CEFR Level A1 - Speaking & Listening - Student's Book - ISBN: 978-1-78164-276-4
- Succeed in IELTS Life Skills - CEFR Level A1 - Speaking & Listening - Self-study Edition - ISBN: 978-1-78164-277-1

The authors and publishers wish to acknowledge the following use of material: 123rf© for the cover photos.

# TABLE OF CONTENTS

## Part 1     IELTS Life Skills Preparation

| | |
|---|---|
| Introduction | page 2 |

### Section A: Basic Grammar & English in Use

| | | |
|---|---|---|
| Unit 1 | Plural nouns | page 6 |
| Unit 2 | Subject pronouns & the verb 'to be' | page 10 |
| Unit 3 | This/that & these/those | page 14 |
| Unit 4 | Who? What? | page 16 |
| Unit 5 | Possessive adjectives & Possessive pronouns | page 18 |
| Unit 6 | The verb 'have got' | page 22 |
| Unit 7 | There is / There are & prepositions of place | page 24 |
| Unit 8 | Countable / uncountable nouns | page 28 |
| Unit 9 | Present continuous | page 32 |
| Unit 10 | How? & Adverbs | page 36 |
| Unit 11 | Present continuous vs present simple | page 38 |
| Unit 12 | Question words | page 40 |

### Section B: Listening Practice

| | | |
|---|---|---|
| Part 1 | Listening to a sentence<br>*Circle the picture that matches what you hear.* | page 44 |
| Part 2 | Listening to a sentence<br>*Circle the best answer to what you hear.* | page 52 |
| Part 3 | Listening to a short conversation<br>*Circle the best answer to the question on the conversation.* | page 54 |

### Section C: Speaking Practice

| | | |
|---|---|---|
| Part 1 | Personal Questions | page 58 |
| Part 2 | Role play | page 59 |
| Part 3 | Topic discussion | page 60 |
| Part 4 | Picture description | page 62 |

## Part 2     IELTS Life Skills Practice

### Section D: Practice Tests

| | | |
|---|---|---|
| Test 1 | theme: Leisure | page 66 |
| Test 2 | theme: Family and Friends | page 69 |
| Test 3 | theme: Work | page 72 |
| Test 4 | theme: Education / Training | page 75 |
| Test 5 | theme: Buying Goods | page 78 |

| | |
|---|---|
| **IELTS Life Skills** Audioscripts | page 81 |
| **IELTS Life Skills** Answer Key | page 85 |

# Succeed in
# IELTS Life Skills A1

## Section A
## Basic Grammar & English in Use

# Unit 1

## Plural nouns

One bus or two buses?

One child or two children?

One baby or two babies?

One box or two boxes?

### Plural nouns

**The regular plural ending is -s:** book - books, pen - pens, banana - bananas, phone - phones.
**Add -es after -o, -s, -ss, -ch, -sh, -x:** tomato - tomatoes, bus - buses, glass - glasses, peach - peaches, dish - dishes, box - boxes.

NOT BY THE RULE: piano - pianos, photo - photos, kangaroo - kangaroos, radio - radios

**Add -s after vowel + y:** day - days, toy - toys.
**Change -f and -fe to -ves:** thief - thieves, knife - knives.
**After consonant + y, change y to -ies:** lady - ladies, family - families.

NOT BY THE RULE: roof - roofs, giraffe - giraffes

# Unit 1

IELTS Life Skills A1:   Grammar & English in Use

## Exercise A
**Write the nouns in the plural.**

balloon - watch - strawberry - kiss - boy - loaf - kangaroo - pen - bush - cow

1. balloons
2. _____
3. _____
4. _____
5. _____
6. _____
7. _____
8. _____
9. _____
10. _____

## Exercise B
**What is in the basket?**

train - piano - ball - plane - doll - lorry - puzzle - guitar - clown - kite

1. two trains
2. _____
3. _____
4. _____
5. _____
6. _____
7. _____
8. _____
9. _____
10. _____

# Unit 1

| irregular nouns | | | |
|---|---|---|---|
| child - children | man - men | woman - women | foot - feet |
| mouse - mice | ox - oxen | fish - fish | goose - geese |
| person - people | tooth - teeth | deer - deer | sheep - sheep |

## Exercise C
**Put the letters in the correct order to form irregular plurals.**

1. ndicerlh    children
2. oepelp    _____
3. mweon    _____
4. enxo    _____
5. esege    _____
6. hetet    _____
7. emn    _____
8. emic    _____
9. etfe    _____
10. peseh    _____

## Exercise D
**Put the nouns in the plural and in the correct column.**

day  church  family  knife  sheep  shelf  city  glass  roof  fox  wolf  tooth
bone  brush  baby  queen  mouse  lady  policeman  potato  radio  leaf  child

| -s | -es | -ies | -ves | irregular |
|---|---|---|---|---|
| days | churches | families | knives | sheep |
|  |  |  |  |  |
|  |  |  |  |  |
|  |  |  |  |  |
|  |  |  |  |  |

IELTS Life Skills A1:   Grammar & English in Use

# Unit 1

## Exercise E
**Write the singular or the plural.**

bird - **birds**

_____ - women

brush - _____

ox - _____

_____ - watches

_____ - people

party - _____

_____ - deer

wolf - _____

businessman - _____

## Exercise F
**Look at the pictures and write the plural nouns.**

1 _____   2 _____   3 _____   4 _____

5 _____   6 _____   7 _____

    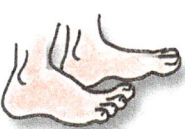

8 _____   9 _____   10 _____

# Unit 2

## subject pronouns & 'to be'

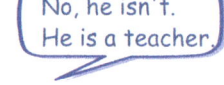

"No, I'm not. I'm a pilot."
"Are you an astronaut?"
"No, he isn't. He is a teacher."
"Is he a businessman?"
"Is she a nurse?"
"No, she isn't. She is a doctor."
"Are they actors?"
"No, they aren't. They're builders."

### subject pronouns

| I | you | he | she | it | we | you | they |
|---|-----|----|----|----|----|----|----|

### the verb 'to be'

| Affirmative | | Interrogative | Negative | | |
|---|---|---|---|---|---|
| **Full form** | **Short form** | | **Full form** | **Short form** | |
| I am | I'm | am I? | I am not | I'm not | |
| you are | you're | are you? | you are not | you're not | you aren't |
| he is | he's | is he? | he is not | he's not | he isn't |
| she is | she's | is she? | she is not | she's not | she isn't |
| it is | it's | is it? | it is not | it's not | it isn't |
| we are | we're | are we? | we are not | we're not | we aren't |
| you are | you're | are you? | you are not | you're not | you aren't |
| they are | they're | are they? | they are not | they're not | they aren't |

IELTS Life Skills A1:    Grammar & English in Use

# Unit 2

## Exercise A
**Put the words in the correct column.**

> Tom - mother - horse - father and I - brother - you and Mum
> Sam and Mary - fireman - Susan - ruler - giraffe - my family and I
> boys - sister - grandmother and grandfather

| He | She | It | We | You | They |
|---|---|---|---|---|---|
| Tom | mother | | | | |

## Exercise B
**Choose the odd one out.**

| 1 | Bill | (sun) | Dad | Mr Jones |
|---|---|---|---|---|
| 2 | door | Tina | ballerina | aunt |
| 3 | apple | orange | cherry | princess |
| 4 | Mary and I | singers | children | girls |

## Exercise C
**Make sentences using the short forms where possible.**

1  I / hungry.                    I'm hungry.
2  it / not / cold.               _____
3  she / not / actress.           _____
4  he / not / strong.             _____
5  I / not / rich.                _____
6  he / happy?                    _____
7  they / not / at work.          _____
8  Svetlana and I / dancers.      _____
9  you / sad?                     _____
10 my parents / not / at home.    _____

# Unit 2

## Exercise D
**Fill in the blanks with am, is or are.**

1 The cake __is__ fantastic.

2 We _____ at the cinema.

3 I _____ a student.

4 You _____ from Greece.

5 The cat _____ in the bedroom.

6 The pens _____ red.

7 The clown _____ funny.

8 She _____ very old.

## Short answers

In **affirmative answers**, always use the full form:
   Yes, I am.
   Yes, he/she/it is.
   Yes, we/you/they are.

In **negative answers**, use the short form:
   No, I'm not.
   No, he/she/it isn't.
   No, we/you/they aren't.

## Exercise E
**Put the sentences into question and negative forms.**

1 The cat is on the roof.  **Is the cat on the roof?**
   **The cat isn't on the roof.**

2 Laura is married.

3 He is in Paris.

4 The children are at school.

5 Zeynep and Tom are friends.

6 It is a star.

7 Helen and Jose are at home.

8 The moon is full.

9 You are a pupil.

10 The pencils are in my bag.

IELTS Life Skills A1:    Grammar  & English in Use

# Unit 2

## Exercise F
**Ask and answer questions.**

1. __Is it__ a parrot?

   __No, it isn't. It's a duck.__

2. _____ a pilot?

   _____

3. _____ bottles?

   _____

4. _____ an actor?

   _____

5. _____ tennis players?

   _____

## Exercise G
**Give short answers.**

1. Are bananas yellow?      __Yes, they are.__

2. Is the sun hot?          _____

3. Are we students?         _____

4. Are you a doctor?        _____

5. Are basketball players short?  _____

6. Is Angelina Jolie Chinese?     _____

# Unit 3

## this/that - these/those

"This is a good book but those on the table are also very nice!"

### this/that - these/those

| Affirmative | Interrogative | Negative | |
|---|---|---|---|
| | | **Full form** | **Short form** |
| this is | is this? | this is not | this isn't |
| that is/that's | is that? | that is not | that isn't |
| these are | are these? | those are not | these aren't |
| those are | are those? | these are not | those aren't |

### Short answers

**Affirmative:** Yes, it is.    **Negative:** No, it isn't.
Yes, they are.    No, they aren't.

14

IELTS Life Skills A1:    Grammar & English in Use

# Unit 3

## Exercise A
**Fill in the blanks with this is / that is or these are / those are.**

1. **A**  ___This is___  a horse and  ___that is___  a zebra.
2. **B**  _____ a dolphin and _____ a whale.
3. **C**  _____ bears and _____ pandas.
4. **D**  _____ ants and _____ bees.
5. **E**  _____ a cow and _____ a bull.
6. **F**  _____ ducks and _____ swans.
7. **G**  _____ wolves and _____ foxes.
8. **H**  _____ a camel and _____ a giraffe.

## Exercise B
**Ask and answer questions.**

1. this / van?            no/lorry     ___Is this a van?___        ___No, it isn't. It's a lorry.___
2. those / kittens?       yes          ___Are those kittens?___    ___Yes, they are.___
3. these / pens?          no/pencils   _____            _____
4. this / tablet?         yes          _____            _____
5. this / TV?             no/computer  _____            _____
6. that / star?           no/comet     _____            _____
7. those / guitars?       yes          _____            _____
8. that / camera?         yes          _____            _____

# Unit 4

## who? - what?

It's Tower Bridge

What's that?

It's Big Ben!

Whats this?

| | |
|---|---|
| **who?** | to ask about people |
| **what?** | to ask about animals, things, jobs |

IELTS Life Skills A1:    Grammar & English in Use

# Unit 4

## Exercise A
**Match the questions with the answers.**

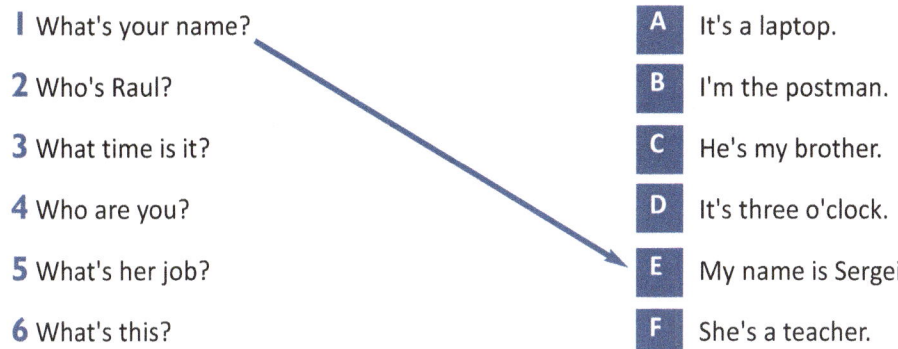

1 What's your name?
2 Who's Raul?
3 What time is it?
4 Who are you?
5 What's her job?
6 What's this?

A It's a laptop.
B I'm the postman.
C He's my brother.
D It's three o'clock.
E My name is Sergei.
F She's a teacher.

## Exercise B
**Fill in the blanks with who or what.**

1 ____What____ is Gayatri?      She's a model.
2 _____ are you?          I'm Cindy Brown.
3 _____ are these?        They're geese.
4 _____ are they?         They're Ibrahim and Wafa.
5 _____ is he?            He's an astronaut.
6 _____ is this?          It's a history book.
7 _____ is Jimmy?         He's my cousin.
8 _____ are those?        They're horses.

## Exercise C
**Ask the questions.**

1 _____What's his name?_____

   His name is *James Bond*.

2 _____

   She's *a pilot*.

3 _____

   This is *a new smartphone*.

4 _____

   She's *my sister*.

5 _____

   A duck is *a bird*.

6 _____

   He's *a singer*.

7 _____

   Those are *foxes*.

8 _____

   They're *my friends*.

17

# Unit 5

## possessive adjectives - possessive pronouns

**Father:** John, this is my smart phone.
**Son:** No dad, it's mine! You can't take it from me!
**Father:** This is mine. Yours is in your room!

| possessive adjectives | possessive pronouns |
|---|---|
| my | mine |
| your | yours |
| his | his |
| her | hers |
| its | ours |
| our | yours |
| your | theirs |
| their | |
| *This is **their** house.* | *This house is **theirs**.* |

**the possessive pronoun its is not used.**

IELTS Life Skills A1:   Grammar & English in Use

# Unit 5

## Exercise A
**Look at the pictures and ask and answer questions about their jobs.**

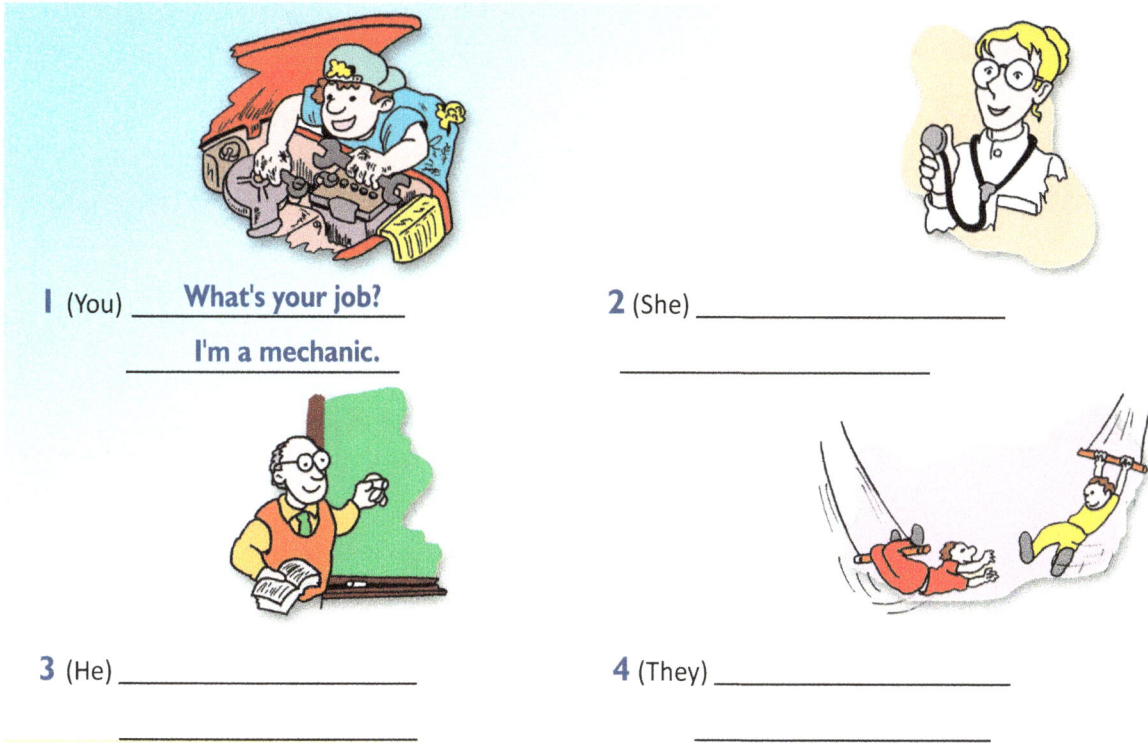

1 (You) ___What's your job?___
   ___I'm a mechanic.___

2 (She) _____
   _____

3 (He) _____
   _____

4 (They) _____
   _____

## Exercise B
**Choose the correct possessive adjective.**

1  The car is new. __b__ colour is red.
   a My            b Its            c Their

2  This is Hoang. _____ dad is an astronaut.
   a Her           b His            c Its

3  The Browns are in the hotel. _____ room is number 5.
   a Their         b Your           c Our

4  I'm a teacher and these are _____ students.
   a its           b our            c my

5  We are from Greece. _____ country is beautiful.
   a Their         b Our            c Its

6  You are a very good student. _____ test results are excellent.
   a Your          b Her            c His

7  She's a pilot. _____ name is Todora.
   a His           b My             c Her

8  We are the new neighbours. _____ names are Omar and Helen.
   a Their         b My             c Our

19

# Unit 5

same pronunciation:
your - you're (you are)
its - it's (it is)
their - they're (they are)

## Exercise C
**Circle the correct answer.**

1. **Their** / They're house is in the country.
2. Your / You're my friend.
3. Look at this cat. Its / It's eyes are green.
4. Their / They're piano players.
5. Is this your / you're apple?
6. Their / They're from Somalia.
7. Its / It's a big bedroom.
8. Their / They're names are Fatimah and Daliyah.

## Exercise D
**Complete the sentences using possessive pronouns.**

1. This is your room. It's ___yours___ .
2. That is her book. It's _____ .
3. Are these your shoes? Are they _____ ?
4. This orange juice is for Pham Tuan. It's _____ .
5. This is our car. It's _____ .
6. Is that their dog? Is it _____ ?
7. Those are my sweets. They're _____ .
8. These are the girls' clothes. They're _____ .

## Exercise E
**Circle the correct word.**

1. **My** / Mine T-shirt is blue.
2. What's your / yours name?
3. These red boots are her / hers .
4. Your / Yours ice-cream is over there.
5. Anna and Natsumi are our / ours friends.
6. Our / Ours motorcycles are in the garage.
7. This is my DVD. Your / Yours is on the table.
8. That i-Phone is my / mine .
9. That large house is their / theirs .
10. Layla is her / hers friend.

IELTS Life Skills A1:   Grammar & English in Use

# Unit 5

## Exercise F
**Fill in the blanks with the correct possessive adjective or pronoun.**

1. Those notebooks are _____mine_____ *(I)*.
2. _____ *(she)* umbrella is yellow.
3. My house is near _____ *(Kento and Katrina)*.
4. _____ *(we)* cat is in the garden.
5. Joe is _____ *(I)* friend.
6. The red Ferrari is _____ *(Hassan)*.
7. This big house is _____ *(Susan and I)*.
8. _____ *(Mr and Mrs Ford)* boat is white.
9. _____ *(wolf)* teeth are sharp.
10. My jacket is green and _____ *(Maria)* is white.

## Exercise G
**Choose the correct answer.**

1. Is _____b_____ office big?
   - a  you
   - b  your
   - c  yours

2. _____ is an actress.
   - a  She
   - b  Her
   - c  Hers

3. This coat is _____.
   - a  I
   - b  my
   - c  mine

4. That's a polar bear. _____ fur is white.
   - a  It
   - b  Its
   - c  It's

5. This is Luca. _____ is from Italy.
   - a  He
   - b  His
   - c  He's

6. That dog is _____ .
   - a  we
   - b  our
   - c  ours

7. _____ mother is an architect.
   - a  I
   - b  My
   - c  Mine

8. Abbas and Hakeem are brothers. _____ parents are doctors.
   - a  They
   - b  Theirs
   - c  Their

# Unit 6

## the verb 'have got'

| the verb 'have got' |||||
|---|---|---|---|---|
| **Affirmative** || **Interrogative** | **Negative** ||
| Full form | Short form | | Full form | Short form |
| I have got | I've got | have I got? | I have not got | I haven't got |
| you have got | you've got | have you got? | you have not got | you haven't got |
| he has got | he's got | has he got? | he has not got | he hasn't got |
| she has got | she's got | has she got? | she has not got | she hasn't got |
| it has got | it's got | has it got? | it has not got | it hasn't got |
| we have got | we've got | have we got? | we have not got | we haven't got |
| you have got | you've got | have you got? | you have not got | you haven't got |
| they have got | they've got | have they got? | they have not got | they haven't got |

### Short answers

**Affirmative:** Yes, I/we/you/they have.    **Negative:** No, I/we/you/they haven't.
Yes, he/she/it has.    No, he/she/it hasn't.

**'got'** is not used in short answers.

# Unit 6

IELTS Life Skills A1:    Grammar & English in Use

## Exercise A
**Fill in the blanks with have got or has got.**

1. Ayumi __has got__ two sisters.
2. Igor and Piotr _____ smartphones.
3. Dina and I _____ the same dress.
4. Husain _____ two cats.
5. Macarena _____ a little boy.
6. I _____ two hamsters at home.
7. This ball _____ blue and red stars.
8. We _____ a new MP3 player.

## Exercise B
**Write the questions.**

1. Alyona / a bike?  __Has Alyona got a bike?__
2. Imran / a computer?  _____
3. Mr and Mrs Thomas / a new car?  _____
4. the house / a big kitchen?  _____
5. she / short hair?  _____
6. you / a brother or a sister?  _____

## Exercise C
**Look at the picture on the first page of this unit and answer the questions.**

1. Has the house got four windows?  __No, it hasn't. It's got six windows.__
2. Has Emma got a diamond ring?  _____
3. Has the boy got a black car?  _____
4. Has the girl got blond hair?  _____
5. Has the house got a garden?  _____
6. Have they got a small house?  _____

## Exercise D
**Answer the following questions.**

1. Have you got a laptop?  _____
2. Have you got a brother or a sister?  _____
3. Has your father got a bike?  _____
4. Has your friend got a car?  _____
5. Have you got sunglasses?  _____
6. What have you got in your room?  _____

# Unit 7

## there is/are & prepositions of place

**Estate Agent:** That's your house, Mr Smith.
There are three bedrooms and a living room. There's a big kitchen and there's also a study room for you.
**Mr Smith:** Is there a dining room?
**Estate Agent:** Yes, there is.
**Mrs Smith:** Are there two bathrooms?
**Estate Agent:** There aren't any bathrooms!
**Mrs Smith:** No bathrooms?
**Estate Agent:** Sorry, there is only one bathroom.

### there is / are

| Affirmative | | Interrogative | Negative | |
|---|---|---|---|---|
| **Full form** | **Short form** | | **Full form** | **Short form** |
| there is | there's | is there? | there is not | there isn't |
| there are | -- | are there? | there are not | there aren't |

### Short answers

**Affirmative:** Yes, there is.
Yes, there are.

**Negative:** No, there isn't.
No, there aren't.

# Unit 7

IELTS Life Skills A1: Grammar & English in Use

## Exercise A
**Fill in the blanks with there is or there are.**

1 __There are__ six cars in the garage.
2 _____ sweets in the fridge.
3 _____ a mouse in the kitchen.
4 _____ ten desks in the office.
5 _____ a swimming pool at the tennis club.
6 _____ a dish on the table.

## Exercise B
**Look at the picture and answer the questions.**

1 Are there two chairs? __No, there aren't. There are two armchairs.__
2 Is there a table? _____
3 Is there a bookcase? _____
4 Are there two sofas? _____
5 Are there four pictures on the walls? _____
6 Is there a window? _____

## Exercise C
**Look at the picture and ask and answer the questions.**

1 __Are there__ two armchairs? __No, there aren't. There are two chairs.__
2 _____ a desk? _____
3 _____ two pictures on the wall? _____
4 _____ two windows? _____
5 _____ a computer? _____
6 _____ five shelves? _____

# Unit 7

## prepositions of place

It's **in** the toy box.   It's **near** the fireplace.   It's **between** the doll and the clown.

It's **next to** the bed.   It's **under** the desk.   It's **behind** the curtain.   It's **in front of** the TV.   It's **on** the shelf.

**where?** to ask about position: *Where is my notebook?*

### Exercise D
Look at the picture. Ask and answer questions.

1. _Where is_ Valeriya?
   _She is behind_ the bookcase.
2. _____ the umbrella?
   _____ the desk and the bed.
3. _____ the dog?
   _____ the bed.
4. _____ the shoes?
   _____ the books.
5. _____ Stanislaw?
   _____ the door.
6. _____ the ruler?
   _____ the vase.
7. _____ the cats?
   _____ the shelf.
8. _____ the keyboard?
   _____ the computer.

# Unit 7

IELTS Life Skills A1:   Grammar  & English in Use

## Exercise E
**Circle the correct preposition.**

1 Your glass is  on / between / (in)  the sink.
2 The books are  between / in / on  the table .
3 The car is  in front of  / under / on  the shop.
4 The teacher is  at / under / next to  the student.
5 Tim is  under / in / at  work.
6 Is your wife  near / at / in  home?
7 There isn't a picture  in / at / on  the wall.
8 My son isn't  on / at / in  school now.

## Exercise F
**Put the words in the correct order.**

1 five / basket / there / apples / in / are / the          There are five apples in the basket.
2 is / next to / a / supermarket / house / our / there    _____
3 dog / a / car / there / the / is / behind               _____
4 near / bus-stop / there / office / is / the / a         _____
5 boats / two / the / are / under / bridge / there        _____
6 on / is / there / moon / the / astronaut / an           _____

## Exercise G
**Look at the picture and fill in the blanks with there's or there are and the correct preposition.**

Leo and Fabian are camping. They are ___in___ their tent _____ the seaside.
_____ a high rock _____ the tent. _____ three birds _____ the rock.
_____ an umbrella _____ the tent. _____ two bikes _____ the tent and the rock.
Oh, no! _____ a ghost _____ their tent.

27

# Unit 8

## countable / uncountable nouns

**Jim:** What have you got to eat?

**Robert:** I've got some cheese, some ham and some bread.

**Jim:** Haven't you got any water?

**Robert:** No, I haven't, but I've got some juice.

**Jim:** How much juice have you got?

**Robert:** I've got one bottle.

**Jim:** Is there any fruit?

**Robert:** Yes, I've got some apples and some grapes.

**Jim:** How many?

**Robert:** Three apples and some grapes.

| countable nouns | uncountable nouns |
|---|---|
| **Use countable** (e.g. girl-girls, egg-eggs) nouns<br>in the **singular** with: a/an, the<br>in the **plural** with: the<br>some/any<br>How many?<br>(not) many<br>a lot of | **Use uncountable** (e.g. bread, juice) with: nouns<br>the<br>some/any<br>How much?<br>(not) much<br>a lot of |

| | |
|---|---|
| **some** in affirmative sentences: | I've got some apples and some cheese. |
| **any** in interrogative and negative sentences: | Have you got any apples?<br>Have you got any fruit?<br>I haven't got any sweets and I haven't got any juice. |
| **How many?** for countable nouns: | How many apples have you got?<br>I've got three. / I haven't got many. / I've got a lot. |
| **How much?** for uncountable nouns: | How much juice have you got?<br>I've got three bottles. / I haven't got much. / I've got a lot. |

IELTS Life Skills A1:   Grammar & English in Use

# Unit 8

## Exercise A
**Put the nouns in the correct column.**

egg - milk - fork - butter - photo - salt - dog - toy
money - time - chair - mother - fruit - sugar

| countable nouns | uncountable nouns |
|---|---|
| egg | |

## Exercise B
**Fill in the blanks with a/an, some or any.**

1  There's __some__ cake on the table.
2  I've got _____ batteries at home.
3  John's got _____ electric guitar.
4  There isn't _____ honey in the jar.
5  There are _____ clouds in the sky.

6  I've got _____ money in my pocket.
7  Is there _____ cold water in the fridge?
8  There aren't _____ tools in the house.
9  There's _____ bird on the roof.
10 Is there _____ van parked in the street?

## Exercise C
**Fill in the blanks with is/isn't, are/aren't.**

1  There _____isn't_____ any coffee in my cup.
2  There _____ some coins in the box.
3  There _____ any chocolate.
4  _____ there any old clothes in this room?
5  _____ there any cake in the cupboard?
6  There _____ some tea in the teapot.

29

# Unit 8

## Exercise D
Look at the pictures and ask and answer questions.

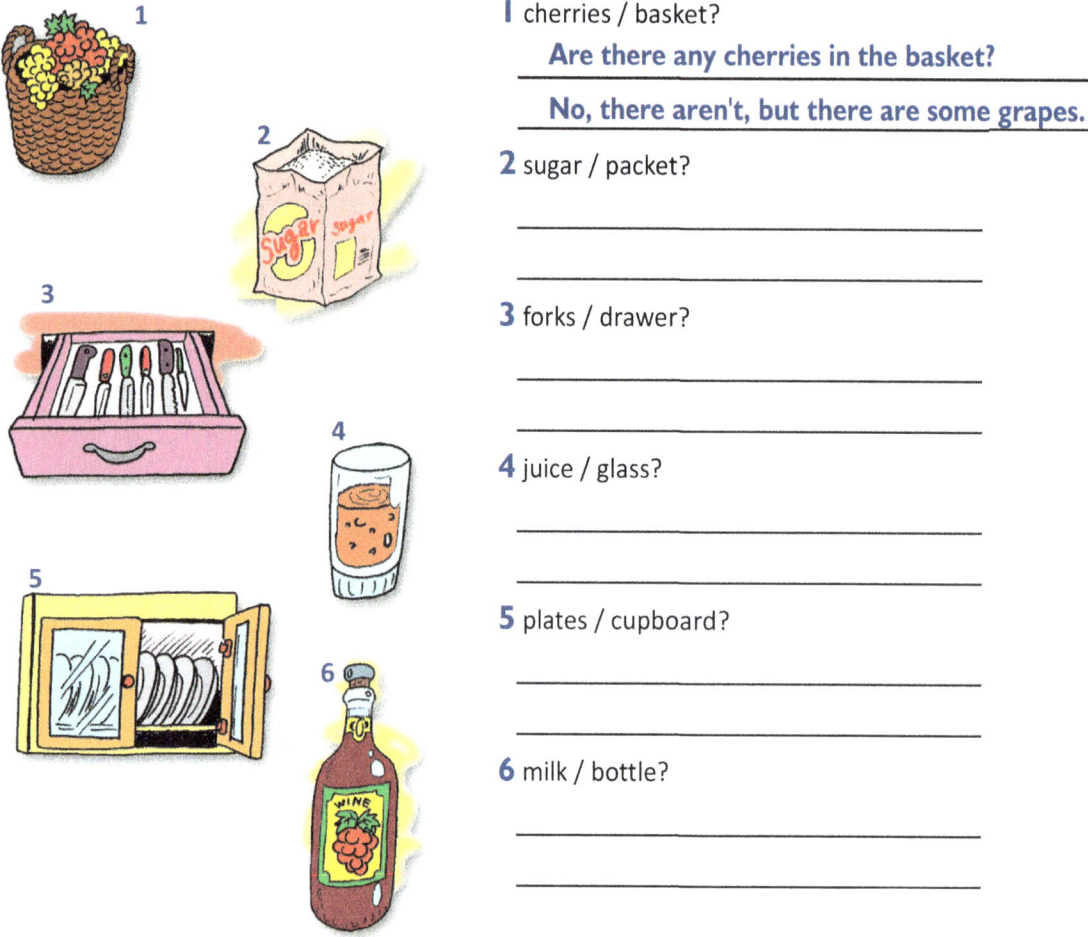

1 cherries / basket?
   Are there any cherries in the basket?
   No, there aren't, but there are some grapes.

2 sugar / packet?
   _____
   _____

3 forks / drawer?
   _____
   _____

4 juice / glass?
   _____
   _____

5 plates / cupboard?
   _____
   _____

6 milk / bottle?
   _____
   _____

## Exercise E
Fill in the blanks with **how much** or **how many**.

1 _____How much_____ sugar is there in the bowl?

2 _____ workers are there in this factory?

3 _____ stars are there in the sky?

4 _____ time have we got?

5 _____ books have you got?

6 _____ lemonade is there in the bottle?

7 _____ money has David got?

8 _____ melons are there in the bag?

*much* and *many* are used most often in negative sentences
and questions and *a lot of* is used in affirmative sentences

IELTS Life Skills A1:   Grammar & English in Use

# Unit 8

## Exercise F
Look at the pictures and write questions and answers.

1 ice cream / bowl
2 bananas / basket
3 coffee / packet
4 crackers / plate
5 rubbish / bin
6 frogs / pond

How much ice cream is there in the bowl? There isn't much.
How many bananas are there in the basket? There are a lot.
_____
_____
_____
_____

> **Use these quantity expressions with uncountable nouns:**
> *a bottle of* water - *a slice of* cake - *a kilo of* flour - *a tin/can of* coke
> *a loaf of* bread - *a cup of* coffee - *a piece of* cheese - *a glass of* wine
> *a bar of* chocolate - *a packet of* rice - *a carton of* juice

*a bottle of* milk - *three bottles of* milk
*a bar of* chocolate - *two bars of* chocolate

## Exercise G
Use the correct quantity expression to describe the pictures.

1  two bars of soap    2 _____    3 _____

4 _____    5 _____    6 _____

31

# Unit 9

## present continuous

My name is John Smith. I'm reporting from the race course at Leeds. The horses are coming into the stadium through the main gate now. They're walking to the starting gates. Photographers are hurrying across the field. People are walking up and down the stairs of the stands. There's a lot of activity here today.

IELTS Life Skills A1:    Grammar & English in Use

# Unit 9

## present continuous

| Affirmative | | Interrogative | Negative | |
|---|---|---|---|---|
| **Full form** | **Short form** | | **Full form** | **Short form** |
| I am eating | I'm eating | am I eating? | I am not eating | I'm not eating |
| you are eating | you're eating | are you eating? | you are not eating | you aren't eating |
| he is eating | he's eating | is he eating? | he is not eating | he isn't eating |
| she is eating | she's eating | is she eating? | she is not eating | she isn't eating |
| it is eating | it's eating | is it eating? | it is not eating | it isn't eating |
| we are eating | we're eating | are we eating? | we are not eating | we aren't eating |
| you are eating | you're eating | are you eating? | you are not eating | you aren't eating |
| they are eating | they're eating | are they eating? | they are not eating | they aren't eating |

### Short answers

**Affirmative:** Yes, I am.
Yes, he/she/it is.
Yes, we/you/they are.

**Negative:** No, I'm not.
No, he/she/it isn't.
No, we/you/they aren't.

## Exercise A
**Write the -ing form of the verbs in the correct column.**

work - come - run - tie - read - study - die - drive - sleep - sit - give
get - go - lie - listen - pull - put - bake - swim - take - watch - write

| working | coming | running | tying |
|---|---|---|---|
| | | | |
| | | | |
| | | | |
| | | | |
| | | | |
| | | | |
| | | | |

# Unit 9

## Exercise B
**Look at the pictures and write sentences in the present continuous.**

1 baby / cry
   **The baby is crying.**

4 girls / watch TV
   _____

2 men / dig / in the garden
   _____

5 baker / make a cake
   _____

3 aeroplane / fly / in the sky
   _____

6 wind / blow
   _____

## Exercise C
**Form sentences in the present continuous.**

1 they / not / dance.
   **They aren't dancing.**

2 she / read / a book?
   _____

3 you / play / chess?
   _____

4 we / study / English.
   _____

5 he / not / sleep.
   _____

6 I / not / work.
   _____

7 they / sit / on the sofa?
   _____

8 she / draw / a picture.
   _____

## Exercise D
Look at the pictures and write questions and answers.

1  Maria / play / with her dolls?
   **Is Maria playing with her dolls?**
   **No, she isn't. She's doing** _____ a puzzle.

4  she / iron / her clothes?
   _____
   _____ a magazine.

2  they / clean / the house?
   _____
   _____ dishes.

5  the / boys / laughing?
   _____
   _____

3  Borys / write / a letter?
   _____
   _____

6  he / do / his homework?
   _____
   _____ a computer game.

# Unit 10

## how? + adverbs

**Doctor:** How is Mr Green doing?

**Nurse:** He's resting quietly.

**Doctor:** How is Mrs Collins's diet?

**Nurse:** Great! She's eating lightly.

**Doctor:** And how is Mr Smith's leg?

**Nurse:** Almost new! He's walking slowly and carefully.

**Doctor:** That's perfect. Good job, Jane.

| adverbs of manner | | | |
|---|---|---|---|
| **Regular** | | **Irregular** | |
| form: adjective+ly | | | |
| **adjective** | **adverb** | **adjective** | **adverb** |
| loud | loudly | good | well |
| nice | nicely | fast | fast |
| beautiful | beautifully | hard | hard |
| careless | carelessly | late | late |

### Note:

angry - angrily    gentle - gently

easy - easily    simple - simply

**How?**  How is he dancing?

# Unit 10

IELTS Life Skills A1:   Grammar & English in Use

## Exercise A
**Change the following adjectives into adverbs.**

| bad | badly | terrible | | quiet | |
| dangerous | | angry | | careful | |
| good | | nice | | fast | |
| awful | | thirsty | | perfect | |

## Exercise B
**Circle the correct word, adjective or adverb.**

1 The boys are singing  happy / (happily).
2 Summer is a  nice / nicely  season for a holiday.
3 The library is a  quiet / quietly  place to read.
4 Sara is dancing  beautiful / beautifully.
5 Lenny and Jabbar are working very  good / well  together.
6 The race car driver is driving  dangerous / dangerously.

## Exercise C
**Put the words in the correct order.**

1 fast / he / driving / is           He is driving fast.
2 badly / Jamal / singing / is      _____
3 now / working / hard / are / they  _____
4 playing / is / awfully / she / today _____
5 walk / not / fast / do            _____
6 shouting / boss / the / is / angrily _____

## Exercise D
**Turn the adjectives into adverbs and ask and answer questions.**

1 How / Jarir / walk?  slow        **How is Jarir walking?  He's walking slowly.**
2 How / Darya / swim?  good        _____
3 How / Takahiro / eat?  hungry    _____
4 How / the boys / run?  quick     _____
5 How / the girl / type?  careless _____
6 How / they / sit?  comfortable   _____

# Unit 11

## present continuous vs present simple

I'm not working this week because I've got a broken arm. I usually do many things at the office every day.

I type, I make coffee, I answer the phone, I make photocopies and I read the mail.

At the moment, my boss is typing, Mary is making coffee and answering the phone, Brian is making photocopies and Robert is reading the emails.

I'm sure they don't like working so hard but I need their help. I know they're doing a lot, but I love doing nothing.

| present continuous | present simple |
| --- | --- |
| He's typing **at the moment**. She's going to work by bus **this week**. | I type **every day**. She **usually** goes to work by car. |

# Unit 11

IELTS Life Skills A1:    Grammar & English in Use

## Exercise A
**Match the questions with the answers.**

1 Does Iskra type fast?
2 Is your sister working?
3 Do they often go out?
4 Are you doing a puzzle?
5 Does your brother smoke?
6 Is he sleeping?

A  No, he doesn't.
B  Yes, she's very busy at the moment.
C  No, she doesn't. She types very slowly.
D  No, only once a month.
E  Yes, so be quiet.
F  Yes, I am. Can you help me?

## Exercise B
**Look at the pictures and answer the questions.**

1 What does Marek usually do?
work/hard    __He usually works hard but_____
lie/in the sun now  __he's lying in the sun now._____

2 What do they do every afternoon?
go/the gym _____
stay/home today _____

3 What does she always do in the morning?
clean/house _____
watch/TV now _____

4 What does she do on Monday mornings?
teach/the college _____
walk/in the park now _____

5 What does Randa sometimes do on Saturday afternoons?
help/mum _____
sleep/at the moment _____

6 What does the cat drink every day?
drink/milk _____
eat/fish today _____

# Unit 12

## question words

| | |
|---|---|
| **Mrs Richards:** | Hello. I'm Mrs Richards and I'm travelling to France. |
| **Check-in assistant:** | Good morning. Who are you visiting in France? |
| **Mrs Richards:** | My nephews. |
| **Check-in assistant:** | Very nice. How many nephews have you got? |
| **Mrs Richards:** | Two. John and Billy. |
| **Check-in assistant:** | When are you coming back? |
| **Mrs Richards:** | In two weeks. |
| **Check-in assistant:** | Where's your ticket? |
| **Mrs Richards:** | Here it is. |
| **Check-in assistant:** | Which suitcases are yours? |
| **Mrs Richards:** | All of them! |

### question words

| | |
|---|---|
| **what?** | to ask about animals, things, jobs, actions |
| **who?** | to ask about people |
| **which?** | to ask about people, animals, things |
| **whose?** | to ask about possession |
| **where?** | to ask about place, direction |
| **when?** | to ask about time |
| **why?** | to ask about reason |
| **how?** | to ask about manner, age, number, quantity, size, weight, length, height |

# Unit 12

IELTS Life Skills A1: Grammar & English in Use

## Exercise A
**Fill in the blanks with the correct question word.**

1  ____What____ is this?                It's a tiger.
2  _____ do you live?            In Bristol.
3  _____ notebook is this?       It's Rihana's.
4  _____ car is yours?           The red one.
5  _____ old are you?            I'm ten.
6  _____ are you doing?          I'm cooking.
7  _____ did he come back?       Yesterday.
8  _____ is she crying?          Because she's sad.
9  _____ is he?                  He's Mr Burns.
10 _____ does she do?            She's a nurse.

## Exercise B
**Match the questions to the answers.**

1  How are you?
2  When is Granny's birthday?
3  Whose bag is this?
4  Where is Izabella?
5  What did you have for dinner?
6  Who's at the door?
7  Which shirt did you buy?
8  Why was she late?

A  It's Klara's.
B  Fish and chips.
C  She's at home.
D  It's on 3rd May.
E  It's the postman.
F  Her car broke down.
G  I'm fine, thank you.
H  The green one.

(1 matched to G)

## Exercise C
**Fill in the blanks with how old, how much, how many, how often, how big, how long.**

1  __How much__ money have we got?        4  _____ is the River Nile?
2  _____ do you go out?            5  _____ people came to the party?
3  _____ is your grandfather?      6  _____ is your room?

## Exercise D
**Read the answers and ask questions with how.**

1  __How often do you go to the gym?_____ I go to the gym **every Friday**.
2  _____ My brother is **seventeen years old**.
3  _____ She's got **£10**.
4  _____ There are **two** computers in the office.
5  _____ Their yacht is **30 metres** long.
6  _____ There are **six** eggs.

# Succeed in
# IELTS Life Skills A1

## Section B
Listening Preparation & Practice

# IELTS LIFE SKILLS  Part 1  LEVEL A1

## Part 1  LISTENING

You hear some sentences twice. Match what you hear with one of the answers. Put a circle round the letter of the correct answer. Now, look at the example. You hear 'It's raining, It's raining', the answer is (b). Ready?

*Example:*

(a)   ((b))   (c)   (d)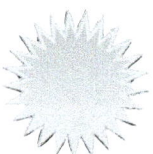

1.  (a)   (b)   (c)   (d)

2.  (a) 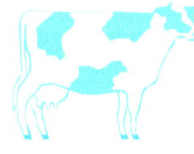  (b)   (c)   (d)

3.  (a)   (b)   (c)   (d)

## SECTION B: Listening Preparation & Practice

# Part 1

4.  (a)   (b)   (c)   (d)

5.  (a) 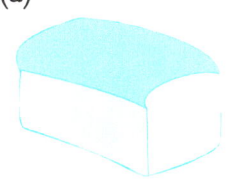  (b) 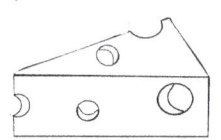  (c)   (d)

6.  (a) TISSA  (b) TESSE  (c) DESSA  (d) TESSA

7.  (a) 30  (b) 31  (c) 13  (d) 33

# IELTS LIFE SKILLS  Part 1  LEVEL A1

8. (a)   (b) 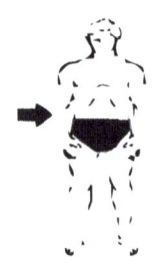  (c)   (d)

9. (a)   (b)   (c)   (d)

10. (a)   (b) 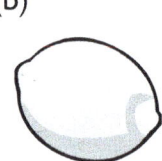  (c) 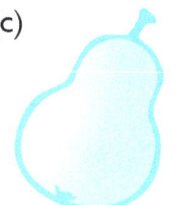  (d)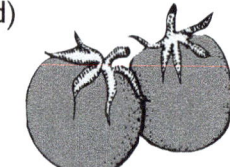

11. (a)   (b)   (c)   (d)

12. (a) ROWOM   (b) ROUAN   (c) ROWAN   (d) RAWAN

**SECTION B: Listening Preparation & Practice**

# Part 1

13. (a)  (b)  (c)  (d)

14. (a)  (b)  (c)  (d)

15. (a)  (b)  (c)  (d)

16. (a)  (b)  (c)  (d)

# IELTS LIFE SKILLS — Part 1 — LEVEL A1

17. (a)  (b)  (c)  (d)

18. (a) ROWOM (b) ROUAN (c) ROWAN (d) RAWAN

19. (a) 15 (b) 5 (c) 55 (d) 50

20. (a)  (b)  (c)  (d)

21. (a)  (b)  (c)  (d)

# Part 1

### SECTION B: Listening Preparation & Practice

22. (a)   (b)   (c)   (d)

23. (a)   (b)  (c) 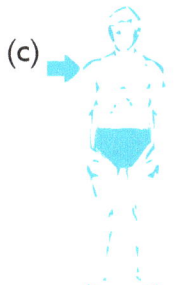  (d)

24. (a)   (b)   (c)  (d)

25. (a) 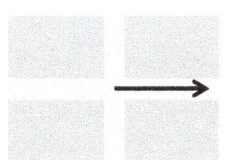  (b) 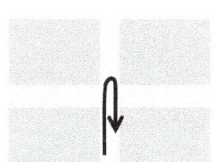  (c) 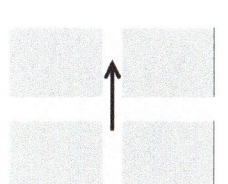  (d)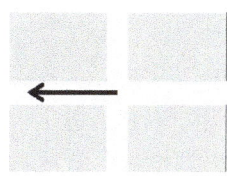

26. (a)   (b)   (c)   (d)

# IELTS LIFE SKILLS — Part 1 — LEVEL A1

27. (a) ROWON  (b) ROUAN  (c) ROWAN  (d) RAWAN

28. (a)   (b)   (c)   (d)

29. (a)   (b)   (c)   (d)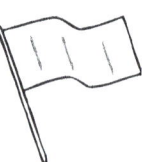

30. (a) 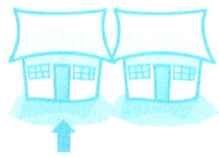  (b)   (c)   (d)

31. (a)  (b)  (c)  (d)

**SECTION B: Listening Preparation & Practice**

# Part 1

32. (a) ROWOM     (b) ROUAN     (c) ROWAN     (d) RAWAN

33. (a)     (b)     (c)     (d)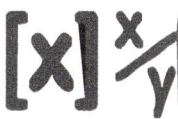

34. (a)    (b)    (c)    (d)

35. (a)     (b)     (c) 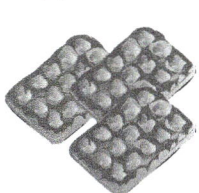    (d)

# IELTS LIFE SKILLS Part 2 LEVEL A1

## Part 2

You hear some sentences twice. Choose the best reply to each sentence. Put a circle round the letter of the best reply. Now, look at the example. Now, look at the example. You hear 'Who's coming tonight?, Who's coming tonight?', the best reply is (b). Ready?

*Example:*
- (a) Tomorrow, I think.
- (b) I certainly am. *(circled)*
- (c) Probably not.
- (d) Why not?

1. 
   - (a) I love you, too.
   - (b) Spiderman 3.
   - (c) Not really.
   - (d) Me, too!

2. 
   - (a) I don't like it.
   - (b) Yes, have some.
   - (c) I want it.
   - (d) No, thank you.

3. 
   - (a) Saturday.
   - (b) Friday, 13th.
   - (c) Tomorrow morning.
   - (d) Eight o'clock.

4. 
   - (a) You're invited, too.
   - (b) Yes, I am!
   - (c) Not until tomorrow.
   - (d) Anne's coming.

5. 
   - (a) You're very welcome.
   - (b) No, thanks.
   - (c) I need some more.
   - (d) I can help.

6. 
   - (a) Very.
   - (b) A few.
   - (c) You are.
   - (d) Maybe I will.

7. 
   - (a) I see you.
   - (b) I can't see it.
   - (c) Here it is.
   - (d) OK, bye for now.

8. 
   - (a) You, too.
   - (b) I can't play.
   - (c) It was fun.
   - (d) Yes, of course!

9. 
   - (a) It's blue and white.
   - (b) It's my jumper.
   - (c) Where is it?
   - (d) Here it is.

10. 
    - (a) You are nice.
    - (b) You, too!
    - (c) I'm not meeting you.
    - (d) Tomorrow morning.

11. 
    - (a) I did it.
    - (b) Don't worry.
    - (c) You, too.
    - (d) I think so.

12. 
    - (a) Her name is Sarah.
    - (b) Yes, two.
    - (c) No, thank you.
    - (d) I am the eldest.

13. 
    - (a) To the zoo.
    - (b) On Friday.
    - (c) At ten o'clock.
    - (d) Maybe later.

14. 
    - (a) I can.
    - (b) It's easy for me.
    - (c) I'm afraid not.
    - (d) You're right.

15. 
    - (a) Yes, that's it.
    - (b) Here she is.
    - (c) Are you sure?
    - (d) Over there.

16. 
    - (a) John's brother.
    - (b) Next January.
    - (c) Over here.
    - (d) 8 and a half.

17. 
    - (a) Hi Jane!
    - (b) Nice to meet you!
    - (c) No, Alice.
    - (d) Here he is.

18. 
    - (a) You do?
    - (b) Eleven, I think.
    - (c) I see.
    - (d) I have not.

19. 
    - (a) That's right!
    - (b) Hi John!
    - (c) No, she's called Jenny.
    - (d) His name is Pat.

20. 
    - (a) Not a lot.
    - (b) I like them.
    - (c) You do.
    - (d) Yesterday.

21. 
    - (a) I love music!
    - (b) She is very good.
    - (c) I agree.
    - (d) Yes, and the piano.

**SECTION B: Listening Preparation & Practice**

# Part 2

22. (a) Are you Jerry?
    (b) Where is Jerry?
    (c) My name is Jane.
    (d) Nice to meet you.

23. (a) I can't.
    (b) Hi Nicola.
    (c) He isn't.
    (d) Sure!

24. (a) Yesterday morning.
    (b) Number 3.
    (c) Three thirty.
    (d) Three and a half.

25. (a) Not today.
    (b) Swimming.
    (c) You can't.
    (d) Yes, please.

26. (a) Thank you very much.
    (b) I like the beach.
    (c) I don't like it.
    (d) Here you go!

27. (a) Here you go!
    (b) I pay two pounds.
    (c) I can.
    (d) It's your pencil.

28. (a) Call 207-3758962.
    (b) I called him.
    (c) Her name's Jill.
    (d) Thomas is his name.

29. (a) Hi Leah!
    (b) Here it is.
    (c) At the dentist's.
    (d) Leah is ten.

30. (a) Not really.
    (b) I played yesterday.
    (c) Well done!
    (d) You are very good.

31. (a) It's right.
    (b) You're not wrong.
    (c) I will. Thank you.
    (d) My tooth hurts.

32. (a) Spain and France.
    (b) On Bark Street.
    (c) At five o'clock.
    (d) Under the big table.

33. (a) She is laughing.
    (b) Are you sure?
    (c) I do.
    (d) I am sad.

34. (a) Friday morning.
    (b) Yesterday.
    (c) Not bad.
    (d) I think so.

35. (a) Last year.
    (b) January 31st.
    (c) Every week.
    (d) Almost.

# IELTS LIFE SKILLS   Part 3   LEVEL A1

## Part 3

You hear some short conversations. Listen to the conversations and choose the best answer to the question. Put a circle round the letter of the correct answer. You hear each conversation twice.

### Conversation 1

The speakers are

a) in a restaurant.
b) at home.
c) at a hotel.
d) in a shop.

### Conversation 2

Tina is

a) at a party.
b) at tennis practice.
c) at home.
d) with the speakers.

### Conversation 3

The woman

a) wins a prize.
b) buys a present.
c) helps the man.
d) gives a lesson.

### Conversation 4

The man is

a) at work.
b) at the woman's house.
c) feeling sick.
d) doing homework.

### Conversation 5

The speakers are

a) parent and child.
b) husband and wife.
c) friends.
d) brother and sister.

### Conversation 6

The man is

a) worried.
b) calm.
c) surprised.
d) happy.

### Conversation 7

The man hurt his

a) neck.
b) back.
c) hand.
d) pencil.

### Conversation 8

What does the man eat?

a) a burger, potatoes and salad
b) a burger and salad
c) a burger and potatoes
d) salad

### Conversation 9

Who is Ms Welsh?

a) the secretary
b) a parent
c) a student
d) a teacher

### Conversation 10

The speakers are talking about

a) cycling.
b) work.
c) driving.
d) colours.

### Conversation 11

The speakers are

a) parent and child.
b) husband and wife.
c) boss and employee.
d) shop assistant and customer.

### Conversation 12

The woman buys some

a) vegetables.
b) fruit.
c) drinks.
d) sweets.

### Conversation 13

Who is Mr Wakefield?

a) Tom's father
b) Tom's teacher
c) the secretary
d) Eric's son

### Conversation 14

The speakers are talking about

a) a car.
b) a house.
c) a person.
d) a room.

### Conversation 15

The speakers are talking about

a) cinema.
b) radio.
c) TV.
d) theatre.

**SECTION B: Listening Preparation & Practice**

# Part 3

## Conversation 16

The speakers are

a) in a restaurant.
b) in a supermarket.
c) at home.
d) at a pizza place.

## Conversation 17

The woman is calling

a) work.
b) her sister, Anna.
c) a restaurant.
d) home.

## Conversation 18

The speakers are

a) mother and son.
b) teacher and student.
c) husband and wife.
d) doctor and parent.

## Conversation 19

The speakers are talking about

a) a radio show.
b) a news programme.
c) going shopping.
d) a film on TV.

## Conversation 20

The speakers are

a) in a bookshop.
b) in a small shop.
c) at the post office.
d) in the street.

## Conversation 21

The speakers are

a) sisters.
b) mother and daughter.
c) shop assistant and customer.
d) friends.

## Conversation 22

The speakers are

a) parent and child.
b) shop assistant and customer.
c) husband and wife.
d) brother and sister.

## Conversation 23

The speakers are

a) at school.
b) in the man's house.
c) in the woman's house.
d) outside.

## Conversation 24

What is the woman paying for?

a) supermarket food
b) a restaurant meal
c) sweets in a shop
d) petrol for a car

## Conversation 25

Where are the speakers?

a) a supermarket
b) a bar
c) a restaurant
d) a corner shop

# Succeed in
# IELTS Life Skills A1

## Section C
Speaking Preparation & Practice

# IELTS LIFE SKILLS  Part 1  LEVEL A1

## Part 1  SPEAKING

In phase 1a of the IELTS Life Skills A1 test you will be asked some personal questions. This part of the preparation helps you to talk a bit about yourself.

Match the following questions to their possible answers. This is just to get you started. Then talk a bit more about each question.

### Set 1

1. Have you got a big or small family?
2. Who's your best friend?
3. Where do you go on holidays?
4. What films do you like?
5. What do you do on weekends?

1 ........
2 ........
3 ........
4 ........
5 ........

a. My family often visits my grandparents in the summer.
b. I come from a small family.
c. My best friend's name is Jennifer.
d. I really like going to the cinema.
e. I mostly watch comedies.

### Set 2

1. Is your bedroom nice?
2. Do you live in a big town?
3. Do you like your school / job?
4. What does your father / mother look like?
5. Do you like to read books?

1 ........
2 ........
3 ........
4 ........
5 ........

a. Actually, my town is quite small.
b. I really enjoy being there but sometimes things are difficult.
c. I really like my bedroom because it's big.
d. They are both tall and thin.
e. Not really; I'm a bit bored.

### Set 3

1. Where do you work / study?
2. How do you get to work / school / college each day?
3. What food do you like?
4. Do you have any pets?
5. Do you like animals?

1 ........
2 ........
3 ........
4 ........
5 ........

a. I work at a local shop and I study Physics.
b. I love all kinds of animals.
c. My favourite is fish and chips.
d. I have a puppy dog called Milo.
e. I have to take the bus.

### Set 4

1. What languages do you speak?
2. Do you like learning English?
3. Are you good at sports?
4. Do you like to watch TV?
5. Who is your favourite singer?

1 ........
2 ........
3 ........
4 ........
5 ........

a. I like surfing on the Internet more than watching TV.
b. I don't think I have one but I like rock singers in general.
c. I really like it but sometimes it's difficult.
d. I am really good at football but nothing else I'm afraid.
e. I speak English and Italian.

### Set 5

1. How often do you go shopping?
2. Do you like concerts?
3. What is your favourite season?
4. Do you like playing board games?
5. Does your house have a nice garden?

1 ........
2 ........
3 ........
4 ........
5 ........

a. I have never been to a concert but I'd love to.
b. Unfortunately not, but I hope I'll have one soon.
c. Yes, it's one of my favourite hobbies.
d. I only go shopping when I really need to buy things.
e. I love summer; I think it's the best time of year.

# SECTION C: Speaking Preparation & Practice

# Part 2

## Part 2

In phase 1b of the IELTS Life Skills A1 test you will be asked some questions. This part of the preparation helps you to answer various questions.

*Match the following questions to their possible answers. This is just to get you started. Then talk a bit more about each question with a partner.*

### Set 1

1. *We are friends.*
   Have you got any pets?

2. *We are friends.*
   Do you want to come to the cinema with me tonight?

3. *I'm in your town. We meet in the street.*
   Excuse me, where's the post office?

1 ………
2 ………
3 ………

a. Oh, sorry! I can't.

b. Unfortunately not.

c. Em, let me think.

### Set 2

1. *We are friends.*
   I'm really hungry. Do you want to have dinner in a restaurant?

2. *We are friends.*
   I'm bored. What is there to watch on TV tonight?

3. *You're my boss. I'm late for work.*
   Sorry I'm late.

1 ………
2 ………
3 ………

a. Where were you then?

b. A new reality show is on tonight.

c. Sure, but where?

### Set 3

1. *We are friends. We are at the tennis club.*
   How often do you come here?

2. *We are friends. I am in your house.*
   What are your plans for tomorrow?

3. *You are the postman/postwoman.*
   Do you have any post for me today?

1 ………
2 ………
3 ………

a. Oh, yes actually.

b. Almost every week, I guess.

c. I don't know yet.

### Set 4

1. *We are friends. We are at a cafe.*
   What do you want to drink?

2. *We are friends.*
   What time is it?

3. *I'm your parent.*
   Why do you want me to give you £5?

1 ………
2 ………
3 ………

a. It's dinner time.

b. I don't know. What about you?

c. Because I really need it.

### Set 5

1. *I work in a shop. You want some milk.*
   Can I help you?

2. *We are friends.*
   Do you like computer games?

3. *I'm a taxi driver. You get in my car.*
   Where do you want to go?

1 ………
2 ………
3 ………

a. Yes, I want some milk.

b. To the airport please.

c. I love them.

# IELTS LIFE SKILLS    Part 3    LEVEL A1

## Part 3

In phase 2b of the IELTS Life Skills A1 test you will be asked to discuss a topic with your partner. This part of the preparation helps you to engage yourself in a conversation.

Talk about the following topics with a partner. If you find it difficult to start, or keep going, you can use the questions given to get more ideas.

### Set 1

**Topics**

**Questions**

**A** What you do at the weekend

What you do at the weekend
- What's your favourite day of the week?
- Where do you usually meet your friends?
- What do you do after school / work?

**B** The music you like

The music you like
- Where do you shop for music?
- When do you listen to music?
- Where do you listen to music?

**C** The weather in your country

The weather in your country
- What's your favourite weather?
- What do you do when it snows?
- What's the weather like today?

### Set 2

**Topics**

**Questions**

**A** Your home town

Your home town
- What fun things can you do there?
- Is it noisy in your home town?
- Is it safe in your town?

**B** Your hobbies

Your hobbies
- Do you and your friends have the same hobbies?
- Are you a good singer?
- Do you play any musical instruments?

**C** Your best friend

Your best friend
- What does he/she look like?
- Do you know him/her a long time?
- What do you not like about him/her?

**SECTION C: Speaking Preparation & Practice**

# Part 3

**Set 3**

| Topics | Questions |
|---|---|
| A  What you take with you on holiday | What you take with you on holiday<br>• What's an important thing to take on holiday?<br>• What clothes are good for a beach holiday?<br>• What clothes are good for a winter holiday? |
| B  Your favourite place | Your favourite place<br>• How often do you go there?<br>• Is it far from your home?<br>• Who do you go there with? |
| C  Your family | Your family<br>• Do you want any (more) brothers or sisters?<br>• What do you like about your parents?<br>• Do you have many aunts and uncles? |

**Set 4**

| Topics | Questions |
|---|---|
| A  What you do on weekday mornings before school / work | What you do on weekday mornings before school / work<br>• (At) what time do you get up?<br>• (At) what time do you go to school / work?<br>• How often do you brush your teeth each day? |
| B  Your teacher / boss | Your teacher / boss<br>• Do you know him or her long?<br>• What do you (not) like about him or her?<br>• About how old is he or she? |
| C  Your favourite subject | Your favourite subject<br>• Do you like Music or Art?<br>• Do you like Maths and/or Science?<br>• Do you prefer History or Geography? |

# IELTS LIFE SKILLS — Part 4 — LEVEL A1

## Part 4

**Throughout the IELTS Life Skills A1 test you will be asked to talk about yourself and about familiar topics. This part of the preparation helps you to practise useful vocabulary (when you describe a picture, when you mention objects, etc) and use appropriate grammar (present continuous, pronouns, prepositions, etc)**

Take a look at the following sets of pictures. Describe the differences that you notice between them. Use appropriate vocabulary and grammar.

### Set 1

Picture A  Picture B

### Set 2

Picture A                    Picture B

**SECTION C: Speaking Preparation & Practice**

# Part 4

**Set 3**     Picture A                                          Picture B

**Set 4**     Picture A                                          Picture B

**Set 5**     Picture A                                          Picture B

63

# Succeed in
# IELTS Life Skills A1

## Section D
Practice Tests

# Test 1

## LEISURE

### A1 Speaking and Listening

**This test should not exceed 18 minutes.**

> *Please note:* With the exception of the Task Sheet in Phase 2a, this sample test frame will be used only by the Examiner. It will not be shown to the candidates.

**4 – 5 minutes** **Phase 1a**

[The Examiner will select questions from those provided in the test pack, in a variety of areas such as name, nationality, work/study, where candidates live and free time activities.]

**PERSONAL QUESTIONS**

1. What's your name?
2. Where do you come from?
3. Where do you live?
4. How old are you?
5. Do you study?
6. What is your job?
7. Do you have any brothers or sisters?
8. Do you have any hobbies?
9. What do you do in your free time?
10. Are you married? Do you have children?

**5 minutes** **Phase 1b**

Now I'd like you to ask each other *[signal]* some questions.

_____ (Candidate A), I'd like you to ask _____ (Candidate B) about his/her hobbies.

_____ (Candidate B), I'd like you to ask _____ (Candidate A) about his/her free time.

Now think about the questions you want to ask. You have one and a half minutes. You can write down your questions if you want to. *[Indicate paper and pencil.]*

If you don't understand, please ask me.

*[Withdraw eye contact to signal start of preparation. Allow 1 ½ minutes for preparation.]*

_____ (Candidate A), are you ready? Please ask _____ (Candidate B) your questions. *[Allow up to 2 minutes.]*

### Candidate A

- Do you have a hobby?
- What are your hobbies?
- What is your favourite hobby?
- Are any of your hobbies expensive?
- Which hobbies are popular in your country?

Thank you.

_____ (Candidate B), are you ready? Please ask _____ (Candidate A) your questions. *[Allow up to 2 minutes.]*

### Candidate B

- Do you have enough free time during the day?
- Do you have free time on Sundays?
- How do you spend your free time?
- How do your friends spend their free time?

Thank you.

## 4 minutes — Phase 2a

In this part of the test, you are going to listen to two recordings and answer some questions. You can make notes *[indicate paper]* if you want to.

You hear two people talking about their favourite sports. *[Hand each candidate the booklet open at the correct page.]* What sport will they play this weekend? Tennis, basketball or football?

**What sport will they play this weekend?**

tennis      basketball      football

Listen to the information. *[Play CD.]*

_____ (Candidate A), in the first recording, what does the man want to play at the weekend? Tennis, basketball or football?

Thank you.

_____ (Candidate B), in the second recording, what does the man want to play at the weekend? Tennis, basketball or football?

Thank you. [Take back booklets.]

Now listen again, and answer these questions.

_____ (Candidate B), in the first recording, how many friends does the man have? [short pause] And when are they going to meet?

_____ (Candidate A), in the second recording, how many men will each team have? [short pause] And how long are they going to play?

[Play CD again: scripts as above. At the end of the recording ask each candidate in turn their two questions again. After **each** question, **wait** for the candidate's response.]

Thank you.

### 3 – 4 minutes     Phase 2b

Now you are going to talk together about your favourite sports. Talk to each other about sports that you like to do and why you like them.

[Repeat if necessary. Withdraw eye contact to signal start of activity.

If necessary prompt candidates with questions from the box below (e.g. if students are experiencing difficulty in continuing the interaction or if they stray from the topic). Adapt if necessary. Encourage candidate-candidate interaction by eliciting agreement or alternative opinions from candidates by asking questions such as "What do you think?", "Tell us what you think.", "And you?"]

> **Favourite sports**
> 
> What is your favourite sport?
> How often do you play your favourite sport?
> Which sport can you play for free?
> Which sport is the most popular in your country?

Thank you. That is the end of the test.
[Ensure candidates DO NOT leave the room with the candidate booklet.]

# Test 2

## FAMILY AND FRIENDS

### A1 Speaking and Listening

**This test should not exceed 18 minutes.**

*Please note:* With the exception of the Task Sheet in Phase 2a, this sample test frame will be used only by the Examiner. It will not be shown to the candidates.

**4 – 5 minutes      Phase 1a**

[The Examiner will select questions from those provided in the test pack, in a variety of areas such as name, nationality, work/study, where candidates live and free time activities.]

**PERSONAL QUESTIONS**
1. What's your name?
2. Where do you come from?
3. Where do you live?
4. How old are you?
5. Do you study?
6. What is your job?
7. Do you have any brothers or sisters?
8. Do you have any hobbies?
9. What do you do in your free time?
10. Are you married? Do you have children?

**5 minutes      Phase 1b**

Now I'd like you to ask each other *[signal]* some questions.

_____ (Candidate A), I'd like you to ask _____ (Candidate B) about his/her family members.

_____ (Candidate B), I'd like you to ask _____ (Candidate A) about his/her best friend.

Now think about the questions you want to ask. You have one and a half minutes. You can write down your questions if you want to. *[Indicate paper and pencil.]*

If you don't understand, please ask me.

*[Withdraw eye contact to signal start of preparation. Allow 1 ½ minutes for preparation.]*

_____ (Candidate A), are you ready? Please ask _____ (Candidate B) your questions. [Allow up to 2 minutes.]

### Candidate A
- Do you have any brothers or sisters? If so, how old are they?
- Do you have any children? If yes, what are their names and ages?
- Do you live with your parents?
- Are friends more important than family? What do you think?

Thank you.

_____ (Candidate B), are you ready? Please ask _____ (Candidate A) your questions. [Allow up to 2 minutes.]

### Candidate B
- Can you describe one of your closest friends?
- Do you have any facebook friends?
- Do you have any long distance friends?
- Do you think it is a good idea to borrow money from a friend? Why or why not?

Thank you.

## 4 minutes — Phase 2a

In this part of the test, you are going to listen to two recordings and answer some questions. You can make notes [indicate paper] if you want to.

You hear two men giving some information about their family. [Hand each candidate the booklet open at the correct page.] What is the information about? Their children, their parents or grandparents?

**What is the information about?**

children

parents

grandparents

Listen to the information. [Play CD.]

_____ (Candidate A), what is the first recording about? Their children, their parents or their grandparents?

Thank you.

_____ (Candidate B), what is the second recording about? Their children, their parents or their grandparents?

Thank you. [Take back booklets.]

Now listen again, and answer these questions.

_____ (Candidate B), in the first recording, how many children does the man have? [short pause] And how old are they?

_____ (Candidate A), in the second recording, how many years ago did the man last speak to his mother? [short pause] And how many children has his father got with his new wife?

[Play CD again: scripts as above. At the end of the recording ask each candidate in turn their two questions again. After **each** question, **wait** for the candidate's response.]

Thank you.

### 3 - 4 minutes     Phase 2b

Now you are going to talk together about your relatives. Talk to each other about the relatives that you have and why you like/dislike them.

[Repeat if necessary. Withdraw eye contact to signal start of activity.

If necessary prompt candidates with questions from the box below (e.g. if students are experiencing difficulty in continuing the interaction or if they stray from the topic). Adapt if necessary. Encourage candidate-candidate interaction by eliciting agreement or alternative opinions from candidates by asking questions such as "What do you think?", "Tell us what you think.", "And you?"]

> **Relatives**
>
> Who is the oldest relative you can remember?
> Who is the most annoying relative?
> Do you think relatives are more important than friends?
> How was your family life when you were a child?

Thank you. That is the end of the test.
[Ensure candidates DO NOT leave the room with the candidate booklet.]

# Test 3

# WORK

## A1 Speaking and Listening

**This test should not exceed 18 minutes.**

> *Please note:* With the exception of the Task Sheet in Phase 2a, this sample test frame will be used only by the Examiner. It will not be shown to the candidates.

### 4 – 5 minutes                    Phase 1a

[The Examiner will select questions from those provided in the test pack, in a variety of areas such as name, nationality, work/study, where candidates live and free time activities.]

**PERSONAL QUESTIONS**

1. What's your name?
2. Where do you come from?
3. Where do you live?
4. How old are you?
5. Do you study?
6. What is your job?
7. Do you have any brothers or sisters?
8. Do you have any hobbies?
9. What do you do in your free time?
10. Are you married? Do you have children?

### 5 minutes                    Phase 1b

Now I'd like you to ask each other *[signal]* some questions.

_____ *(Candidate A)*, I'd like you to ask _____ *(Candidate B)* about his/her current job.

_____ *(Candidate B)*, I'd like you to ask _____ *(Candidate A)* about his/her first job.

Now think about the questions you want to ask. You have one and a half minutes. You can write down your questions if you want to. *[Indicate paper and pencil.]*

If you don't understand, please ask me.

*[Withdraw eye contact to signal start of preparation. Allow 1 ½ minutes for preparation.]*

_____ (Candidate A), are you ready? Please ask _____ (Candidate B) your questions. *[Allow up to 2 minutes.]*

## Candidate A

- Can you describe your job?
- Are you happy with your salary?
- Do you have to work overtime? If so, do you get extra money?
- Do you like your boss?

Thank you.

_____ (Candidate B), are you ready? Please ask _____ (Candidate A) your questions. *[Allow up to 2 minutes.]*

## Candidate B

- What was your first job?
- How did you find it?
- How old were you when you got your first job?
- Can you describe some of the people you worked with?

Thank you.


**4 minutes         Phase 2a**

In this part of the test, you are going to listen to two recordings and answer some questions.
You can make notes *[indicate paper]* if you want to.

You hear two people talking about their jobs. *[Hand each candidate the booklet open at the correct page.]*
What do they do for a living? Teacher, waiter, or doctor?

**What do they do for a living?**

teacher

waiter

doctor

Listen to the information. *[Play CD.]*

**IELTS - Life Skills A1**      **Practice Test 3**      **Speaking & Listening**

_____ (Candidate A), in the first recording, what does the woman do for a living? Teacher, waiter, or doctor?

Thank you.

_____ (Candidate B), in the second recording, what does the woman do for a living? Teacher, waiter, or doctor?

Thank you. *[Take back booklets.]*

Now listen again, and answer these questions.

_____ (Candidate B), in the first recording, how many students does the woman have? *[short pause]* And what is the first subject she is going to teach?

_____ (Candidate A), in the second recording, what is the main job duty of the woman? *[short pause]* And how many old people does she have to take care of?

*[Play CD again: scripts as above. At the end of the recording ask each candidate in turn their two questions again. After **each** question, **wait** for the candidate's response.]*

Thank you.

### 3 - 4 minutes      Phase 2b

Now you are going to talk together about job choices that people make. Talk to each other about how people choose a particular job and the motives they have for doing so.

*[Repeat if necessary. Withdraw eye contact to signal start of activity.*

*If necessary prompt candidates with questions from the box below (e.g. if students are experiencing difficulty in continuing the interaction or if they stray from the topic). Adapt if necessary. Encourage candidate-candidate interaction by eliciting agreement or alternative opinions from candidates by asking questions such as "What do you think?", "Tell us what you think.", "And you?"]*

> **Job choices**
> 
> How does money affect your job decisions?
> How do your desires affect your career options?
> What job would you like to do?
> Would you like to be the boss?

Thank you. That is the end of the test.
*[Ensure candidates DO NOT leave the room with the candidate booklet.]*

# Test 4

# EDUCATION/TRAINING

## A1 Speaking and Listening

**This test should not exceed 18 minutes.**

*Please note:* With the exception of the Task Sheet in Phase 2a, this sample test frame will be used only by the Examiner. It will not be shown to the candidates.

### 4 – 5 minutes      Phase 1a

[The Examiner will select questions from those provided in the test pack, in a variety of areas such as name, nationality, work/study, where candidates live and free time activities.]

**PERSONAL QUESTIONS**

1. What's your name?
2. Where do you come from?
3. Where do you live?
4. How old are you?
5. Do you study?
6. What is your job?
7. Do you have any brothers or sisters?
8. Do you have any hobbies?
9. What do you do in your free time?
10. Are you married? Do you have children?

### 5 minutes      Phase 1b

Now I'd like you to ask each other *[signal]* some questions.

_____ *(Candidate A)*, I'd like you to ask _____ *(Candidate B)* about his/her school years.

_____ *(Candidate B)*, I'd like you to ask _____ *(Candidate A)* about his/her favourite teacher.

Now think about the questions you want to ask. You have one and a half minutes. You can write down your questions if you want to. *[Indicate paper and pencil.]*

If you don't understand, please ask me.

*[Withdraw eye contact to signal start of preparation. Allow 1 ½ minutes for preparation.]*

# IELTS - Life Skills A1     Practice Test 4     Speaking & Listening

_____ (Candidate A), are you ready? Please ask _____ (Candidate B) your questions. *[Allow up to 2 minutes.]*

## Candidate A

- Did you go to a private or a public secondary school?
- Which was your favourite subject?
- Did you have to wear a uniform while in school?
- Do you enjoy studying English?

Thank you.

_____ (Candidate B), are you ready? Please ask _____ (Candidate A) your questions. *[Allow up to 2 minutes.]*

## Candidate B

- Can you describe your favourite teacher?
- What did you like most about him/her?
- What subject did she teach?
- Do you like to have a male or female teacher?

Thank you.

## 4 minutes     Phase 2a

In this part of the test, you are going to listen to two recordings and answer some questions. You can make notes *[indicate paper]* if you want to.

You hear two people talking about their education. *[Hand each candidate the booklet open at the correct page.]* What level of education are they referring to? Primary, secondary or tertiary (university-level)?

**What level of education are they referring to?**

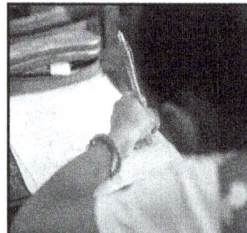  

**primary**        **secondary**        **tertiary**

Listen to the information. *[Play CD.]*

_____ (Candidate A), in the first recording, what level of education is the man referring to? Primary, secondary or tertiary?

Thank you.

_____ (Candidate B), in the second recording, what level of education is the man referring to? Primary, Secondary or Tertiary?

Thank you. *[Take back booklets.]*

Now listen again, and answer these questions.

_____ (Candidate B), in the first recording, how many professors did the man have? *[short pause]* And where did he get a job?

_____ (Candidate A), in the second recording, how many best friends did the man have in high school? *[short pause]* And what was his favourite subject?

*[Play CD again: scripts as above. At the end of the recording ask each candidate in turn their two questions again. After **each** question, **wait** for the candidate's response.]*

Thank you.

### 3 - 4 minutes     Phase 2b

Now you are going to talk together about your country's tertiary education system. Talk to each other about the types of universities/colleges that exist in your country and what they offer.

*[Repeat if necessary. Withdraw eye contact to signal start of activity.*

*If necessary prompt candidates with questions from the box below (e.g. if students are experiencing difficulty in continuing the interaction or if they stray from the topic). Adapt if necessary. Encourage candidate-candidate interaction by eliciting agreement or alternative opinions from candidates by asking questions such as "What do you think?", "Tell us what you think.", "And you?"]*

> **Tertiary Education**
>
> Are there private as well as public universities in your country?
> Do students have to pay money to go to university?
> Did your studies help you find a good job?
> Is a university degree important if you want to get a job?

Thank you. That is the end of the test.
*[Ensure candidates DO NOT leave the room with the candidate booklet.]*

# Test 5

## BUYING GOODS

### A1 Speaking and Listening

**This test should not exceed 18 minutes.**

*Please note:* With the exception of the Task Sheet in Phase 2a, this sample test frame will be used only by the Examiner. It will not be shown to the candidates.

**4 – 5 minutes**                **Phase 1a**

[The Examiner will select questions from those provided in the test pack, in a variety of areas such as name, nationality, work/study, where candidates live and free time activities.]

> **PERSONAL QUESTIONS**
>
> 1. What's your name?
> 2. Where do you come from?
> 3. Where do you live?
> 4. How old are you?
> 5. Do you study?
> 6. What is your job?
> 7. Do you have any brothers or sisters?
> 8. Do you have any hobbies?
> 9. What do you do in your free time?
> 10. Are you married? Do you have children?

**5 minutes**                **Phase 1b**

Now I'd like you to ask each other *[signal]* some questions.

_____ (Candidate A), I'd like you to ask _____ (Candidate B) about his/her shopping habits.

_____ (Candidate B), I'd like you to ask _____ (Candidate A) about his/her favourite shops.

Now think about the questions you want to ask. You have one and a half minutes. You can write down your questions if you want to. *[Indicate paper and pencil.]*

If you don't understand, please ask me.

*[Withdraw eye contact to signal start of preparation. Allow 1 ½ minutes for preparation.]*

# IELTS - Life Skills A1 — Practice Test 5 — Speaking & Listening

_____ (Candidate A), are you ready? Please ask _____ (Candidate B) your questions. *[Allow up to 2 minutes.]*

## Candidate A

- Do you enjoy shopping?
- What kind of things do you often buy?
- Who do you often go shopping with?
- Are you good at saving money?

Thank you.

_____ (Candidate B), are you ready? Please ask _____ (Candidate A) your questions. *[Allow up to 2 minutes.]*

## Candidate B

- For which person do you often buy things?
- About how much money did you spend on presents for others, last year?
- Do you ever buy very expensive things?
- What's your favourite place to shop?

Thank you.

### 4 minutes — Phase 2a

In this part of the test, you are going to listen to two recordings and answer some questions. You can make notes *[indicate paper]* if you want to.

You hear two people talking about their shopping habits. *[Hand each candidate the booklet open at the correct page.]* Where are they going shopping? To the supermarket, the computer store or the garden centre?

**Where are they going shopping?**

supermarket

computer store

garden centre

Listen to the information. *[Play CD.]*

_____ (Candidate A), in the first recording, where is the man going for shopping? To the supermarket, the computer store or the garden centre?

Thank you.

_____ (Candidate B), in the second recording, where is the man going for shopping? To the supermarket, the computer store or the garden centre?

Thank you. *[Take back booklets.]*

Now listen again, and answer these questions.

_____ (Candidate B), in the first recording, what is the man going to buy? *[short pause]* And to which supermarket are they going today?

_____ (Candidate A), in the second recording, to which computer store is the man going? *[short pause]* And what is his daughter going to buy?

*[Play CD again: scripts as above. At the end of the recording ask each candidate in turn their two questions again. After **each** question, **wait** for the candidate's response.]*

Thank you.

### 3 - 4 minutes        Phase 2b

Now you are going to talk together about your money habits. Talk to each other about how and where you spend your money.

*[Repeat if necessary. Withdraw eye contact to signal start of activity.*

*If necessary prompt candidates with questions for the box below (e.g. if students are experiencing difficulty in continuing the interaction or if they stray from the topic). Adapt if necessary. Encourage candidate-candidate interaction by eliciting agreement or alternative opinions from candidates by asking questions such as "what "What do you think?", "Tell us what you think.", "And you?"]*

> **Money habits**
> 
> Are you good at saving money?
> Do you compare prices at different shops when you shop?
> Do you ever give money to charity?
> Do you have a credit card? Do you use it often?

Thank you. That is the end of the test.
*[Ensure candidates DO NOT leave the room with the candidate booklet.]*

## IELTS Life Skills - Level A1   Audioscripts

## Section B - Listening Preparation & Practice

## Part 1

You are going to hear some sentences twice. Match what you hear with one of the answers. Put a circle round the letter of the correct answer. Now, look at the example. (15 seconds.) You hear 'It's raining, It's raining', the answer is (b). Ready?

### Number 1. Number 1.
[pause 6 seconds]
He likes to go driving.
He likes to go driving.
[pause 10 seconds]

### Number 2. Number 2.
[pause 6 seconds]
That's a donkey.
That's a donkey.
[pause 10 seconds]

### Number 3. Number 3.
[pause 6 seconds]
I like your trousers.
I like your trousers.
[pause 10 seconds]

### Number 4. Number 4.
[pause 6 seconds]
I'm angry with John.
I'm angry with John.
[pause 10 seconds]

### Number 5. Number 5.
[pause 6 seconds]
I had egg for breakfast.
I had egg for breakfast.
[pause 10 seconds]

### Number 6. Number 6.
[pause 6 seconds]
Her name is Dessa - that's D-e-s-s-a.
Her name is Dessa - that's D-e-s-s-a.
[pause 10 seconds]

### Number 7. Number 7.
[pause 6 seconds]
He is thirty years old.
He is thirty years old.
[pause 10 seconds]

### Number 8. Number 8.
[pause 6 seconds]
I hurt my shoulder.
I hurt my shoulder.
[pause 10 seconds]

### Number 9. Number 9.
[pause 6 seconds]
The football costs seventeen pounds.
The football costs seventeen pounds.
[pause 10 seconds]

### Number 10. Number 10.
[pause 6 seconds]
Can you get me a lemon, please?
Can you get me a lemon, please?
[pause 10 seconds]

### Number 11. Number 11.
[pause 6 seconds]
I'll sit on the armchair.
I'll sit on the armchair.
[pause 10 seconds]

### Number 12. Number 12.
[pause 6 seconds]
His name is Rowan - that's R-o-w-a-n.
His name is Rowan - that's R-o-w-a-n.
[pause 10 seconds]

### Number 13. Number 13.
[pause 6 seconds]
Let's play football.
Let's play football.
[pause 10 seconds]

### Number 14. Number 14.
[pause 6 seconds]
My favourite subject is geography.
My favourite subject is geography.
[pause 10 seconds]

### Number 15. Number 15.
[pause 6 seconds]
I have a pet fish.
I have a pet fish.
[pause 10 seconds]

### Number 16. Number 16.
[pause 6 seconds]
I have some new socks.
I have some new socks.
[pause 10 seconds]

### Number 17. Number 17.
[pause 6 seconds]
The film made me feel afraid.
The film made me feel afraid.
[pause 10 seconds]

### Number 18. Number 18.
[pause 6 seconds]
My surname's Smithers - that's S-m-i-t-h-e-r-s.
My surname's Smithers - that's S-m-i-t-h-e-r-s.
[pause 10 seconds]

### Number 19. Number 19.
[pause 6 seconds]
She is fifteen years old.
She is fifteen years old.
[pause 10 seconds]

### Number 20. Number 20.
[pause 6 seconds]
I don't want any potatoes, thank you.
I don't want any potatoes, thank you.
[pause 10 seconds]

### Number 21. Number 21.
[pause 6 seconds]
It's both cloudy and sunny.
It's both cloudy and sunny.
[pause 10 seconds]

### Number 22. Number 22.
[pause 6 seconds]
Thirteen pounds, please.
Thirteen pounds, please.
[pause 10 seconds]

### Number 23. Number 23.
[pause 6 seconds]
My arm hurts a lot.
My arm hurts a lot.
[pause 10 seconds]

### Number 24. Number 24.
[pause 6 seconds]
I love small chocolate buns.
I love small chocolate buns.
[pause 10 seconds]

### Number 25. Number 25.
[pause 6 seconds]
Turn around and go back.
Turn around and go back.
[pause 10 seconds]

### Number 26. Number 26.
[pause 6 seconds]
I think it's in the cupboard.
I think it's in the cupboard.
[pause 10 seconds]

### Number 27. Number 27.
[pause 6 seconds]
My road is called Chase - that's C-h-a-s-e.
My road is called Chase - that's C-h-a-s-e.
[pause 10 seconds]

### Number 28. Number 28.
[pause 6 seconds]
I was playing tennis.
I was playing tennis.
[pause 10 seconds]

### Number 29. Number 29.
[pause 6 seconds]
She's on the phone.
She's on the phone.
[pause 10 seconds]

### Number 30. Number 30.
[pause 6 seconds]
My flag has three squares.
My flag has three squares.
[pause 10 seconds]

### Number 31. Number 31.
[pause 6 seconds]
I can see one house only.
I can see one house only.
[pause 10 seconds]

### Number 32. Number 32.
[pause 6 seconds]
His name is Leary - that's L-e-a-r-y.
His name is Leary - that's L-e-a-r-y.
[pause 10 seconds]

### Number 33. Number 33.
[pause 6 seconds]
That will be thirty-two pounds, please.
That will be thirty-two pounds, please.
[pause 10 seconds]

### Number 34. Number 34.
[pause 6 seconds]
I love history class!
I love history class!
[pause 10 seconds]

### Number 35. Number 35.
[pause 6 seconds]
Auntie gave me sweets.
Auntie gave me sweets.
[pause 10 seconds]
That is the end of Part One.

# Part 2

You are going to hear some sentences twice. Choose the **best** reply to each sentence. Put a circle around the letter of the **best** reply. Now, look at the example. (15 seconds.) You hear 'Who's coming tonight?, Who's coming tonight?', the **best** reply is (b). Ready?

**Number 1. Number 1.**
[pause 6 seconds]
I love that movie!
I love that movie!
[pause 10 seconds]

**Number 2. Number 2.**
[pause 6 seconds]
Would you like some more?
Would you like some more?
[pause 10 seconds]

**Number 3. Number 3.**
[pause 6 seconds]
What time is it, now?
What time is it, now?
[pause 10 seconds]

**Number 4. Number 4.**
[pause 6 seconds]
Are you coming to the party?
Are you coming to the party?
[pause 10 seconds]

**Number 5. Number 5.**
[pause 6 seconds]
Thanks for all your help.
Thanks for all your help.
[pause 10 seconds]

**Number 6. Number 6.**
[pause 6 seconds]
Are you sure?
Are you sure?
[pause 10 seconds]

**Number 7. Number 7.**
[pause 6 seconds]
See you on Friday!
See you on Friday!
[pause 10 seconds]

**Number 8. Number 8.**
[pause 6 seconds]
Can I play, too?
Can I play, too?
[pause 10 seconds]

**Number 9. Number 9.**
[pause 6 seconds]
Where's my jumper?
Where's my jumper?
[pause 10 seconds]

**Number 10. Number 10.**
[pause 6 seconds]
Hello! Nice to meet you.
Hello! Nice to meet you.
[pause 10 seconds]

**Number 11. Number 11.**
[pause 6 seconds]
I'm really sorry.
I'm really sorry.
[pause 10 seconds]

**Number 12. Number 12.**
[pause 6 seconds]
Have you any brothers or sisters?
Have you any brothers or sisters?
[pause 10 seconds]

**Number 13. Number 13.**
[pause 6 seconds]
Where are you going?
Where are you going?
[pause 10 seconds]

**Number 14. Number 14.**
[pause 6 seconds]
Can I come, too?
Can I come, too?
[pause 10 seconds]

**Number 15. Number 15.**
[pause 6 seconds]
Where's the train station?
Where's the train station?
[pause 10 seconds]

**Number 16. Number 16.**
[pause 6 seconds]
How old is Toby?
How old is Toby?
[pause 10 seconds]

**Number 17. Number 17.**
[pause 6 seconds]
Is she called Jane?
Is she called Jane?
[pause 10 seconds]

**Number 18. Number 18.**
[pause 6 seconds]
Do you know the answer?
Do you know the answer?
[pause 10 seconds]

**Number 19. Number 19.**
[pause 6 seconds]
So your name is John?
So your name is John?
[pause 10 seconds]

**Number 20. Number 20.**
[pause 6 seconds]
Do you play football?
Do you play football?
[pause 10 seconds]

**Number 21. Number 21.**
[pause 6 seconds]
Can you play the guitar?
Can you play the guitar?
[pause 10 seconds]

**Number 22. Number 22.**
[pause 6 seconds]
Jerry, this is my sister Michelle.
Jerry, this is my sister Michelle.
[pause 10 seconds]

**Number 23. Number 23.**
[pause 6 seconds]
Can Nicola come, too?
Can Nicola come, too?
[pause 10 seconds]

**Number 24. Number 24.**
[pause 6 seconds]
At what time is the show on?
At what time is the show on?
[pause 10 seconds]

**Number 25. Number 25.**
[pause 6 seconds]
Where are you going?
Where are you going?
[pause 10 seconds]

**Number 26. Number 26.**
[pause 6 seconds]
Would you like a drink?
Would you like a drink?
[pause 10 seconds]

**Number 27. Number 27.**
[pause 6 seconds]
Can I have a pencil, please?
Can I have a pencil, please?
[pause 10 seconds]

**Number 28. Number 28.**
[pause 6 seconds]
What is your brother called?
What is your brother called?
[pause 10 seconds]

**Number 29. Number 29.**
[pause 6 seconds]
Where is Leah?
Where is Leah?
[pause 10 seconds]

**Number 30. Number 30.**
[pause 6 seconds]
Are you good at tennis?
Are you good at tennis?
[pause 10 seconds]

**Number 31. Number 31.**
[pause 6 seconds]
Is there something wrong?
Is there something wrong?
[pause 10 seconds]

**Number 32. Number 32.**
[pause 6 seconds]
Where is your house?
Where is your house?
[pause 10 seconds]

**Number 33. Number 33.**
[pause 6 seconds]
Why are you crying?
Why are you crying?
[pause 10 seconds]

**Number 34. Number 34.**
[pause 6 seconds]
When is the test?
When is the test?
[pause 10 seconds]

**Number 35. Number 35.**
[pause 6 seconds]
When is your birthday?
When is your birthday?
[pause 10 seconds]
That is the end of Part Two.

# Part 3

*You're going to hear some short conversations. Listen to the conversations and choose the **best answer** to the question. Put a circle round the letter of the correct answer. You hear each conversation twice. Look at the question for Conversation One*

## Conversation 1
**F:** What a lovely meal!
**M:** Mmmm. Yes! Delicious! Better than a take-away meal.
**F:** And probably most restaurant food, too!
**M:** Well done, mum!
**F:** What a fantastic meal!
*[Pause: Wait ten seconds before repeating.]*
*[Pause: Wait ten seconds before going to the next conversation.]*
*Now, look at the question for Conversation 2 (10 seconds).*

## Conversation 2
**M:** This is a super party. But where's Tina?
**F:** She's not here.
**M:** Oh, how come? Is she at tennis practice?
**F:** I don't think she's feeling well.
**M:** She's at home in bed? How terrible!
**F:** She's missing all the fun!
*[Pause: Wait ten seconds before repeating.]*
*[Pause: Wait ten seconds before going to the next conversation.]*
*Now, look at the question for Conversation 3 (10 seconds).*

## Conversation 3
**M:** Well done, Helen! You won! First prize; here you go.
**F:** Oh, thank you!
**M:** How do you feel?
**F:** Fantastic! I'm really happy!
**M:** Great job!
*[Pause: Wait ten seconds before repeating.]*
*[Pause: Wait ten seconds before going to the next conversation.]*
*Now, look at the question for Conversation 4 (10 seconds).*

## Conversation 4
**F:** I'm going soon. Do you want to come with me?
**M:** Em ... I do, but I'm too busy.
**F:** Still working on the school project?
**M:** Yes... It's taking a long time.
**F:** Oh well. Never mind.
*[Pause: Wait ten seconds before repeating.]*
*[Pause: Wait ten seconds before going to the next conversation.]*
*Now, look at the question for Conversation 5 (10 seconds).*

## Conversation 5
**F:** What does Toby want for his birthday?
**M:** He didn't say.
**F:** Mum thinks we must get him a new football.
**M:** What does dad think?
**F:** I never asked him.
*[Pause: Wait ten seconds before repeating.]*
*[Pause: Wait ten seconds before going to the next conversation.]*
*Now, look at the question for Conversation 6 (10 seconds).*

## Conversation 6
**M:** Oh no!
**F:** What's wrong?
**M:** I forgot - we have a test today.
**F:** I'm surprised, Rex. You don't forget things often.
**M:** What will I do?
**F:** Calm down! The teacher will understand.
*[Pause: Wait ten seconds before repeating.]*
*[Pause: Wait ten seconds before going to the next conversation.]*
*Now, look at the question for Conversation 7 (10 seconds).*

## Conversation 7
**M:** Ouch! Hey; watch it!
**F:** Sorry! Did I hit you?
**M:** In the back of the neck. What is that in your hand anyway?
**F:** A pencil.
**M:** Well it sure hurt....
*[Pause: Wait ten seconds before repeating.]*
*[Pause: Wait ten seconds before going to the next conversation.]*
*Now, look at the question for Conversation 8 (10 seconds).*

## Conversation 8
**M:** Can I have a burger, please?
**F:** Would you like potatoes or salad with that?
**M:** Both please.
**F:** That'll cost extra.
**M:** Just salad then.
*[Pause: Wait ten seconds before repeating.]*
*[Pause: Wait ten seconds before going to the next conversation.]*
*Now, look at the question for Conversation 9 (10 seconds).*

## Conversation 9
**F:** Hello. Can I help you?
**M:** Yes, can I see Ms Welsh, please?
**F:** Do you have an appointment?
**M:** No, but I have a sick note for my son.
**F:** I'm afraid she's in class at the moment.
**M:** Oh. Can I give it to you?
**F:** Of course. I'm the secretary.
*[Pause: Wait ten seconds before repeating.]*
*[Pause: Wait ten seconds before going to the next conversation.]*
*Now, look at the question for Conversation 10 (10 seconds).*

## Conversation 10
**F:** That's a nice car! I love the colour!
**M:** Thank you. I use it for work. Do you drive?
**F:** I'm learning. For now, I get the bus, usually.
**M:** I also like cycling, but I prefer the car now.
*[Pause: Wait ten seconds before repeating.]*
*[Pause: Wait ten seconds before going to the next conversation.]*
*Now, look at the question for Conversation 11 (10 seconds).*

## Conversation 11
**W:** Can I help you, sir?
**M:** Yes, I need to buy a birthday present for my boss.
**W:** Man or woman?
**M:** Woman.
**W:** Does she have kids?
**M:** Three.
**W:** How about this?
**M:** Perfect!
*[Pause: Wait ten seconds before repeating.]*
*[Pause: Wait ten seconds before going to the next conversation.]*
*Now, look at the question for Conversation 12 (10 seconds).*

## Conversation 12
**M:** Can I help you?
**F:** Three large potatoes, please.
**M:** Certainly. Anything else?
**F:** Yes, some carrots, thank you.
**M:** There you go. That's two pounds fifty.
*[Pause: Wait ten seconds before repeating.]*
*[Pause: Wait ten seconds before going to the next conversation.]*
*Now, look at the question for Conversation 13 (10 seconds).*

## Conversation 13
**F:** Hello.
**M:** Hello. Can I speak to Mr Wakefield?
**F:** What's your name, please?
**M:** Eric Letram, Tom Letram's father.
**F:** One moment. Mr Wakefield is expecting your call.
*[Pause: Wait ten seconds before repeating.]*
*[Pause: Wait ten seconds before going to the next conversation.]*
*Now, look at the question for Conversation 14 (10 seconds).*

## Conversation 14
**F:** How old is it?
**M:** 20 years, but it looks like new.
**F:** Is it big?
**M:** Yeah. Two floors and eight rooms.
**F:** Are you happy there?
**M:** The kids love it.
*[Pause: Wait ten seconds before repeating.]*
*[Pause: Wait ten seconds before going to the next conversation.]*
*Now, look at the question for Conversation 15 (10 seconds).*

## Conversation 15
**F:** I was watching Channel 6.
**M:** Not anymore!
**F:** Change it back!
**M:** What's on that channel anyway?
**F:** A show called *Big Brother*.
*[Pause: Wait ten seconds before repeating.]*
*[Pause: Wait ten seconds before going to the next conversation.]*
*Now, look at the question for Conversation 16 (10 seconds)*

## Conversation 16
**F:** Hello, this is Amy at Italia Place.
**M:** Hi. Can I order two large cheese pizzas, please?
**F:** Drinks?
**M:** No, thank you. How long will it take?
**F:** For collection or delivery?
**M:** For delivery, please.
**F:** The food will be at your house in about 25 minutes.
*[Pause: Wait ten seconds before repeating.]*
*[Pause: Wait ten seconds before going to the next conversation.]*
*Now, look at the question for Conversation 17 (10 seconds).*

# IELTS Life Skills - Level A1 — Audioscripts

## Conversation 17
**M:** Hello, John speaking. Can I help you?
**F:** Yes, I want to book a table, please.
**M:** For how many people?
**F:** Let's see ... mum, dad, my sister, Anna - and me, of course!
**M:** For this evening?
**F:** Yes. After work - about 6:30.
**M:** Certainly.
*[Pause: Wait ten seconds before repeating.]*
*[Pause: Wait ten seconds before going to the next conversation.]*
Now, look at the question for Conversation 18 (10 seconds).

## Conversation 18
**M:** Is there someone at home to look after her?
**F:** My husband works all day. I do, too.
**M:** An older brother or sister, perhaps?
**F:** Yes, of course; Tom can do it. Will she be okay?
**M:** Of course, it's just a bad cold.
*[Pause: Wait ten seconds before repeating.]*
*[Pause: Wait ten seconds before going to the next conversation.]*
Now, look at the question for Conversation 19 (10 seconds).

## Conversation 19
**F:** What time does it start?
**M:** Six thirty.
**F:** Oh no! We'll miss the start.
**M:** But only five minutes or so.
**F:** I guess. It's three hours long, right?
**M:** That's what it said just now on the radio.
*[Pause: Wait ten seconds before repeating.]*
*[Pause: Wait ten seconds before going to the next conversation.]*
Now, look at the question for Conversation 20 (10 seconds).

## Conversation 20
**F:** Can I help you?
**M:** Yes; this newspaper and a bottle of milk, please.
**F:** Is that everything?
**M:** Em ... do you sell stamps?
**F:** We don't have any now. Sorry.
**M:** Never mind; there's a post office across the road.
**F:** One pound seventy-five, please.
**M:** Thank you.
*[Pause: Wait ten seconds before repeating.]*
*[Pause: Wait ten seconds before going to the next conversation.]*
Now, look at the question for Conversation 21 (10 seconds).

## Conversation 21
**F:** I need a dress for the party.
**F2:** Why don't you ask your sister?
**F:** We, em, had a fight.
**F2:** Well, I'm the wrong size, Mary. I can't help.
**F:** Oh... I'll just have to buy one then.
**F2:** There's a nice shop on the corner.
*[Pause: Wait ten seconds before repeating.]*
*[Pause: Wait ten seconds before going to the next conversation.]*
Now, look at the question for Conversation 22 (10 seconds).

## Conversation 22
**M:** When are you getting married?
**F:** Early June. Oh, this is nice.
**M:** Quite expensive, though.
**F:** How much?
**M:** £3,000.
**F:** For a dress? Hmm. That is a lot. My mum and dad can buy it!
*[Pause: Wait ten seconds before repeating.]*
*[Pause: Wait ten seconds before going to the next conversation.]*
Now, look at the question for Conversation 23 (10 seconds).

## Conversation 23
**M:** Hello Miss Wilson!
**F:** Hello Jake! I didn't know you live round here.
**M:** Yes, just up the road. And you, Miss?
**F:** I go walking here all the time.
**M:** Well, see you at school, Miss!
**F:** Goodbye Jake!
*[Pause: Wait ten seconds before repeating.]*
*[Pause: Wait ten seconds before going to the next conversation.]*
Now, look at the question for Conversation 24 (10 seconds).

## Conversation 24
**F:** How much should I put in?
**M:** £20; it's a long drive.
**F:** OK, I'll pay in the shop.
**M:** OK, but be quick, because we'll be late for our meal.
**F:** We have a lot of time; don't worry. The dinner is at 8 o'clock.
*[Pause: Wait ten seconds before repeating.]*
*[Pause: Wait ten seconds before going to the next conversation.]*
Now, look at the question for Conversation 25 (10 seconds).

## Conversation 25
**F:** What did you order?
**M:** A beer.
**F:** No food? Let me see the menu.
**M:** They only have snacks - you know, crisps and peanuts.
**F:** Oh, I see.
*[Pause: Wait ten seconds before repeating.]*
*[Pause: 10 seconds]*
That is the end of Part Three.

# Section D - Practice Tests

## Test 1 - Leisure
**Listening script 1:**
I am very good at tennis, but I want to play football with my five friends this weekend. My friends, Sam, David, Nick, John and George are very good football players. They play football four times a week. They can teach me how to play. We are going to meet at the park this Saturday morning at ten o' clock.

**Listening script 2:**
I want to play basketball with my friends this weekend. We usually play tennis but this time we have a new ball and want to play basketball. We are going to have two teams, each having four men and we are going to play for about forty minutes.

## Test 2 - Family and friends
**Listening Script 1:**
I have two children. My son, the oldest, is 12 years old. His name is Andrew. My daughter's name is Alicia and she is 7 years old. They started at a new school in September and want to join some new clubs. They both like rock music and they can play the guitar.

**Listening script 2:**
The last time I spoke to my mother was 10 years ago. Our relationship is very bad after her divorce with my dad. Later, my dad decided to get married with another woman and now they have two girls, Mary and Linda.

## Test 3 - Work
**Listening Script 1:**
Jessica's mother is a doctor but Jessica teaches 3rd grade at Brighton College. Her class has 22 children; 13 boys and 9 girls. Today, she is teaching Maths and the children want to learn how to solve problems. The next subject she is going to teach is English and then she has a class meeting with the other teachers.

**Listening script 2:**
Samantha works at a hospital in London. She is a doctor and works with twenty nurses. She looks after fifty old people. What she mainly does is take blood. She talks with each patient and with all the nurses and therapists.

## Test 4 - Education/Training
**Listening Script 1:**
I still remember my University years at Lancaster. I studied Medicine for 3 years. I had 12 professors, who were really good. When I graduated, I applied for a job at Lancaster hospital and then I started working there.

**Listening script 2:**
I feel my high school years are the most memorable. I had two best friends, Anna and David and we had three fantastic years. Our favourite subject was Maths and I really feel we have learnt a lot. I can say that High School was really great.

## Test 5 - Buying Goods
**Listening Script 1:**
Today I'm going to buy vegetables and meat with my mother. We normally go to Desco supermarket but today we are going to Waitrest. It is near our house. My mother's boss is coming to our house for dinner tonight. So everything has to be perfect in order for my mum to get the promotion.

**Listening script 2:**
My computer broke down and I need to buy a new one. I will go to Laptops Direct and I will also buy a printer. My daughter will come with me because she needs to buy a tablet and my wife will come as well because she wants to buy a new computer screen.

# IELTS Life Skills - Level A1    Answer Key

## Section A:
**BASIC GRAMMAR & ENGLISH IN USE**

### UNIT 1
**Ex.A:**
2. watches   3. strawberries
4. kisses   5. boys   6. loaves
7. kangaroos   8. pens   9. bushes
10. cows

**Ex.B:**
2. two pianos   3. four balls
4. three planes   5. three dolls
6. two lorries   7. four puzzles
8. two guitars   9. three clowns
10. two kites

**Ex.C:**
2. people   3. women   4. oxen
5. geese   6. teeth   7. men   8. mice
9. feet   10. sheep

**Ex.D:**
-s: roofs, bones, queens, radios
-es: glasses, foxes, brushes, potatoes
-ies: cities, babies, ladies
-ves: shelves, wolves, leaves
irregular: teeth, mice, policemen, children

**Ex.E:**
woman - women,  brush - brushes, ox - oxen,  watch - watches,
person - people,  party - parties,
deer - deer,  wolf - wolves,
businessman - businessmen

**Ex.F:**
2. desks   3. keys   4. shelves
5. mice   6. tomatoes   7. fish   8. kings
9. cherries   10. feet

### UNIT 2
**Ex.A:** *He:* brother, fireman
*She:* Susan, sister
*It:* horse, ruler, giraffe
*We:* father and I, my family and I
*You:* you and Mum
*They:* Sam and Mary, boys, grandmother and grandfather

**Ex.B:** 2. door   3. princess   4. Mary and I

**Ex.C:**
2. It's not/It isn't cold.
3. She's not/She isn't an actress.
4. He's not/He isn't strong.
5. I'm not rich.
6. Is he happy?
7. They're not/They aren't at work.
8. Svetlana and I are dancers.
9. Are you sad?
10. My parents are not at home.
**Ex.D:** 2. are   3. am   4. are   5. is
6. are   7. is   8. is

**Ex.E:**
2. Is Laura married? / Laura isn't married.
3. Is he in Paris? / He isn't in Paris.
4. Are the children at school? / The children aren't at school.
5. Are Zeynep and Tom friends? / Zeynep and Tom aren't friends.
6. Is it a star? / It isn't a star.
7. Are Helen and Jose at home? / Helen and Jose aren't at home.
8. Is the moon full? / The moon isn't full.
9. Are you a pupil? / You aren't a pupil.
10. Are the pencils in my bag? / The pencils aren't in my bag.

**Ex.F:**
2. Is she / Yes, she is.
3. Are they / No, they aren't. They're glasses.
4. Is he / No, he isn't. He's a singer.
5. Are they / Yes, they are.

**Ex.G:**
2. Yes, it is.   3. Yes, we are.
4. No, I'm not. (Yes, I am)
5. No, they aren't.   6. No, she isn't.

### UNIT 3
**Ex.A:**
2. This is ... that is
3. These are ... those are
4. These are ... those are
5. This is ... that is
6. These are ... those are
7. These are ... those are
8. This is ... that is

**Ex.B:**
3. Are these pens? / No, they aren't. They're pencils.
4. Is this a tablet? / Yes, it is.
5. Is this a TV? / No, it isn't. It's a computer.
6. Is that a star? / No, it isn't. It's a comet.
7. Are those guitars? / Yes, they are.
8. Is that a camera? / Yes, it is.

### UNIT 4
**Ex.A:** 2.C   3.D   4.B   5.F   6.A

**Ex.B:**
2. Who
3. What
4. Who
5. What
6. What
7. Who
8. What

**Ex.C:**
2. What is she?
3. What is this?
4. Who is she?
5. What is a duck?
6. What is he?
7. What are those?
8. Who are they?

### UNIT 5
**Ex.A:**
2. What's her job? / She's a doctor.
3. What's his job? / He's a teacher.
4. What's their job? / They're acrobats.

**Ex.B:** 2.b   3.a   4.c   5.b   6.a   7.c   8.c

**Ex.C:**
2. You're   3. Its   4. They're
5. your   6. They're   7. It's   8. Their

**Ex.D:**
2. hers   3. yours   4. his   5. ours
6. theirs   7. mine   8. theirs

**Ex.E:**
2. your   3. hers   4. Your   5. our
6. Our   7. Yours   8. mine   9. theirs
10. her

**Ex.F:**
2. Her   3. theirs   4. Our   5. my
6. his   7. ours   8. Their   9. Its   10. hers

**Ex.G:** 2.a   3.c   4.b   5.a   6.c   7.b   8.c

### UNIT 6
**Ex.A:**
2. have got
3. have got
4. has got
5. has got
6. have got
7. has got
8. have got

**Ex.B:**
2. Has Imran got a computer?
3. Have Mr and Mrs Thomas got a new car?
4. Has the house got a big kitchen?
5. Has she got short hair?
6. Have you got a brother or a sister?

**Ex.C:**
2. Yes, she has.
3. No, he hasn't. He's got a red car.
4. Yes, she has.
5. Yes, it has.
6. No, they haven't. They've got a big house.

**Ex.D:** 2. *{Students give their own answers}*

# IELTS Life Skills - Level A1　　　　　Answer Key

## UNIT 7
**Ex.A:**
2. There are   3. There is
4. There are   5. There is   6. There is

**Ex.B:**
2. Yes, there is.   3. No, there isn't.   4. Yes, there are.   5. No, there aren't. There are two pictures on the walls.
6. Yes, there is.

**Ex.C:**
2. Is there / Yes, there is.
3. Are there / No, there aren't.
There is one picture on the wall.
4. Are there / No, there aren't.
There is one window.
5. Is there / No, there isn't.
6. Are there / No, there aren't.
There are four shelves.

**Ex.D:**
2. Where is / It's between
3. Where is / It's under
4. Where are / They're next to
5. Where is / He's at
6. Where is / It's in
7. Where are / They're on
8. Where is / It's in front of

**Ex.E:**
2. on   3. in front of   4. next to
5. at   6. at   7. on   8. at

**Ex.F:** 2. There is a supermarket next to our house.
3. There is a dog behind the car.
4. There is a bus stop near the office.
5. There are two boats under the bridge.
6. There is an astronaut on the moon.

**Ex.G:**
at, There's, next to, There are, on, There's, in front of, There are, between, There's, behind

## UNIT 8
**Ex.A:**
*countable nouns:* fork, photo, dog, toy, chair, mother
*uncountable nouns:* milk, butter, salt, money, time, fruit, sugar

**Ex.B:**
2. some   3. an   4. any   5. some
6. some   7. any   8. any   9. a   10. a

**Ex.C:** 2. are   3. isn't   4. Are   5. Is   6. is

**Ex.D:**
2. Is there any sugar in the packet? / Yes, there is.
3. Are there any forks in the drawer? / No, there aren't, but there are some knives.
4. Is there any juice in the glass? /
Yes, there is.
5. Are there any plates in the cupboard? / Yes, there are.
6. Is there any milk in the bottle? /
No, there isn't, but there is some wine.

**Ex.E:**
2. How many   3. How many
4. How much   5. How many
6. How much   7. How much
8. How many

**Ex.F:**
3. How much coffee is there in the packet?   There is a lot.
4. How many crackers are there in the plate?   There aren't many.
5. How much rubbish is there in the bin?   There is a lot.
6. How many frogs are there in the pond?   There aren't many.

**Ex.G:**
2. a piece of chalk
3. three cartons of milk
4. three cups of tea
5. four tins of beer
6. a slice of bread

## UNIT 9
**Ex.A:**
*working:* reading, studying, sleeping, going, listening, pulling, watching
*coming:* driving, giving, baking, taking, writing
*running:* sitting, getting, putting, swimming
*tying:* dying, lying

**Ex.B:**
2. The men are digging in the garden.
3. The aeroplane is flying in the sky.
4. The girls are watching TV.
5. The baker is making a cake.
6. The wind is blowing.

**Ex.C:** 2. Is she reading a book?
3. Are you playing chess?
4. We are studying English.
5. He isn't sleeping.
6. I'm not working.
7. Are they sitting on the sofa?
8. She's drawing a picture.

**Ex.D:**
2. Are they cleaning the house?
No, they aren't. They're washing...
3. Is Borys writing a letter? Yes, he is.
4. Is she ironing her clothes?
No, she isn't. She's reading...
5. Are the boys laughing? Yes, they are.
6. Is he doing his homework?
No, he isn't. He's playing

## UNIT 10
**Ex.A:**
2. terrible - terribly   quiet - quietly   dangerous - dangerously
angry - angrily   careful - carefully   good - well
nice - nicely   fast - fast   awful - awfully   thirsty - thirstily
perfect - perfectly

**Ex.B:**
2. nice   3. quiet   4. beautifully
5. well   6. dangerously

# IELTS Life Skills - Level A1 — Audioscripts

## Answer Key

**Ex.C:**
2. Jamal is singing badly.
3. They are working hard now.
4. She is playing awfully today.
5. Do not walk fast.
6. The boss is shouting angrily.

**Ex.D:**
2. How is Darya swimming?
She's swimming well.
3. How is Takahiro eating?
He's eating hungrily.
4. How are the boys running?
They're running quickly.
5. How is the girl typing?
She's typing carelessly.
6. How are they sitting?
They're sitting comfortably.

# UNIT 11

**Ex.A:** 2.B  3.D  4.F  5.A  6.E

**Ex.B:**
2. They go to the gym every afternoon but they're staying at home today.
3. She always cleans the house in the morning but she's watching TV now.
4. She teaches at the college on Monday mornings but she's walking in the park now.
5. Randa sometimes helps her mum on Saturday afternoons but she's sleeping at the moment.
6. It drinks milk every day but it's eating fish today.

# UNIT 12

**Ex.A:**
2. Where  3. Whose  4. Which  5. How
6. What   7. When   8. Why
9. Who    10. What

**Ex.B:** 2.D  3.A  4.C  5.B  6.E  7.H  8.F

**Ex.C:**
2. How often  3. How old
4. How long   5. How many  6. How big

**Ex.D:**
2. How old is your brother?
3. How much money has she got?
4. How many computers are there in the office?
5. How long is their yacht?
6. How many eggs are there?

## Section B:
### LISTENING PREPARATION & PRACTICE

**PART 1**
1.c  2.b  3.d  4.a  5.c  6.c  7.a  8.c  9.a
10.b  11.b  12.c  13.d  14.b  15.c  16.b
17.c  18.a  19.a  20.d  21.c  22.b  23.d
24.d  25.b  26.b  27.a  28.d  29.d  30.c
31.b  32.a  33.a  34.b  35.a

**PART 2**
1.d  2.d  3.d  4.b  5.a  6.a  7.d  8.d
9.d  10.b  11.b  12.b  13.a  14.c  15.d
16.d  17.c  18.b  19.a  20.a  21.d  22.d
23.d  24.c  25.b  26.a  27.a  28.d  29.c
30.a  31.d  32.b  33.d  34.a  35.b

**PART 3**
1.b  2.c  3.a  4.d  5.d  6.a  7.a  8.b  9.d
10.c  11.d  12.a  13.b  14.b  15.c  16.c
17.c  18.d  19.d  20.b  21.d  22.b  23.d
24.d  25.b

## Section C:
### SPEAKING PRACTICE

**PART 1**
Set 1:  1.b  2.c  3.a  4.e  5.d
Set 2:  1.c  2.a  3.b  4.d  5.e
Set 3:  1.a  2.e  3.c  4.d  5.b
Set 4:  1.e  2.c  3.d  4.a  5.b
Set 5:  1.d  2.a  3.e  4.c  5.b

**PART 2**
Set 1:  1.b  2.a  3.c
Set 2:  1.c  2.b  3.a
Set 3:  1.b  2.c  3.a
Set 4:  1.b  2.a  3.c
Set 5:  1.a  2.c  3.b

## Section D:
### IELTS Life Skills - Level A1 PRACTICE TESTS

**TEST 1**
Phase 2a:
- football
- basketball
- Five / This Saturday morning at 10 o'clock
- four / about 40 minutes

**TEST 2**
Phase 2a:
- children
- parents
- two / twelve and seven
- ten / two

**TEST 3**
Phase 2a:
- teacher
- doctor
- 22 / Maths
- taking blood / 50

**TEST 4**
Phase 2a:
- tertiary
- secondary
- 12 / Lancaster Hospital
- 2 / Maths

**TEST 5**
Phase 2a:
- to the supermarket
- to the computer store
- vegetables and meat / Waitrest
- Laptop Direct / a tablet

Lightning Source UK Ltd.
Milton Keynes UK
UKOW07f0657150916

283035UK00007B/20/P